MORE WORDS THAT SELL

A THESAURUS TO HELP YOU PROMOTE YOUR PRODUCTS, SERVICES, AND IDEAS

Richard Bayan

McGraw·Hill

New York   Chicago   San Francisco   Lisbon   London   Madrid   Mexico City
Milan   New Delhi   San Juan   Seoul   Singapore   Sydney   Toronto

Library of Congress Cataloging-in-Publication Data

Bayan, Richard.
    More words that sell : a thesaurus to help you promote your products, services,
and ideas / Richard Bayan.
        p.   cm.
    Includes bibliographical references and index.
     ISBN 0-07-141853-9
      1. Advertising copy.   2. Advertising—Terminology.   3. Vocabulary
I. Title.

HF5825.B248   2004
659.1′01′4—dc21   2003046054

To Anne, my wife and playmate,
with all my love and admiration

ISBN 0-07-141853-9

McGraw-Hill books are available at special quantity discounts to use as premiums and
sales promotions, or for use in corporate training programs. For more information, please
write to the Director of Special Sales, Professional Publishing, McGraw-Hill, Two Penn
Plaza, New York, NY 10121-2298. Or contact your local bookstore.

This book is printed on acid-free paper.

CONTENTS

CONTENTS

ACKNOWLEDGMENTS

No book is ever a solo achievement, even when the name of a single author graces the cover. Let me take this opportunity to thank my various collaborators and coconspirators.

I'm grateful to my original editor, Danielle Egan-Miller, for suggesting this project and guiding me through the early stages. Her successor, Denise Betts, took the reins with grace and good humor; she would have won my loyalty even if she hadn't told me that my introduction was one of the best she's ever read. I owe a further debt of gratitude to editorial team leader Craig Bolt and his skilled staff, who managed to transform my manuscript into a book despite a hailstorm of last-minute author's alterations. Thanks, too, to Scott Rattray for his sleek and elegant interior design.

My wife, Anne, deserves credit for tolerating my eccentric work habits, offering friendly encouragement, and donating her limited free time to tackle my household chores during the deadline crunch. Our cat, Henry, and our German shepherd, Frieda, also provided critical emotional support.

Finally, I would like to thank all the anonymous copywriters whose skill as phrasemakers and persuaders provided me with the foundation for this book. These hardworking scribes—these professional Cyranos—woo customers with their words but never receive due credit for their eloquence. I'd like to give them credit right here, right now.

INTRODUCTION

Back in 1984, when I was a young and underpaid copywriter toiling in the lower-middle regions of the publishing industry, a former colleague came to me with an intriguing challenge. My mission, if I chose to accept it, was to compile a thesaurus of words and phrases used in advertising.

It seemed like a worthwhile project, and I ran with it. I looked forward to creating a useful little idea-starter for my fellow copywriters—at least the direct-mail, in-house breed scattered here and there at isolated outposts across our republic. If the book sold a thousand copies and I could use it in my own work, I would be content.

As it turned out, *Words That Sell* sold way more than a thousand copies. In fact, it became one of those well-thumbed reference books that adorn the desks of hardworking folks everywhere. Its enduring popularity amazed me.

What also amazed me was the range of people who responded to the book: not only advertising copywriters like me, but marketing managers, small business owners, trainers, corporate CEOs, public relations professionals—anybody who did anything that required the right words to put it across.

Words That Sell had made its mark, and I was pleased. But I wasn't completely satisfied. I had written the book under a tight deadline, and I knew it had just scratched the surface. I wanted a chance to dig deeper.

My publisher gave me that chance by commissioning me to write the present book. I wondered how to create a second *Words That Sell* without perplexing the people who owned the first book. It's not easy to juggle two reference books that serve the same purpose. Imagine if Roget had written a second thesaurus, forcing you to shuttle back and forth between the two volumes!

No, *More Words That Sell* would have to be fundamentally different from its predecessor. I would let the original book stand as a thesaurus for all-purpose advertising and promotional messages. The new book would take the concept to the next level: specialized lists of words and phrases you can use to fine-tune your copy and target it to specific audiences.

Ideally, you'll be using the two books as partners, dipping into *Words That Sell* for your basic features and benefits, then turning to *More Words That Sell* to refine your copy for your intended market. But you can also use each volume independently.

Think of *More Words That Sell* as your special-purpose word-and-phrase resource, the book that takes up where *Words That Sell* leaves off. To my knowledge, no other book supplies you with the tools you need to target your copy so precisely.

Here's what you'll find in *More Words That Sell*:

- Lists of words and phrases for niche markets like business-to-business, nonprofit, young people, seniors, subscriptions, and technology
- Unique lists of "upscale," "emotional," "cerebral," and other special-impact words. Use these lists to tweak your copy for the precise tone you want—not an easy task if you try it on your own.
- In-depth lists of colors, flavors, fragrances, sounds, and textures to give your copy more vivid sensory appeal. (The color list also comes in handy if you need to select just the right names for your product color choices.)
- Words and phrases for writing concise but effective classified ads—including *personals*. (Who said advertising had to be all business?!)
- Extensive lists of powerful verbs that add muscle to your copy
- Personal qualities arranged by category—ideal for updating your résumé, writing letters of recommendation, or finding the right words for annual employee reviews
- A long list of *negative* qualities for knocking the competition or conjuring up nightmare scenarios that your product or service can fix
- A powerful selection of "magic-response words"—those *can't-miss* advertising perennials that boost results by appealing to basic human needs

How have I organized all these lists? At first I considered arranging them by category (special markets, "tweakers," sensory words, verbs, personal qualities, and so on), which would have given the book an admirably logical structure. But logic doesn't always make sense—in books, advertising, or real life. In the end, it seemed more practical to organize *More Words That Sell* alphabetically from start to finish—from "Business-to-Business" to "Youth Market." That way, you can go straight to the list you want instead of having to guess the category and turn to the relevant section of the book.

Keep in mind that the words and phrases in each list aren't necessarily synonymous. (This book is less a thesaurus than a series of word menus.) I've simply gathered the most useful expressions under each heading to help you choose the most appropriate words.

At first glance, there seems to be no discernible pattern to the way I've arranged the contents of each list. But if you look more closely, you might notice an underlying stream-of-consciousness approach that sweeps you along from one concept to the next. As in the original *Words That Sell*, I've taken care to see that closely related words and phrases "clump together" within each list. That makes it a lot easier for you to compare your choices.

You'll notice, too, that many of the phrases contain blanks or trail off in ellipses (. . .) where the phrase breaks off. Here I've supplied you with the *pattern* of a phrase that you can adapt to your needs by filling in the missing words or fleshing out the sentence as you see fit.

For special help with copy techniques (including writing for the Internet), turn to the four appendixes at the back of the book. I've also supplied you with a list of books for further reading. All the titles are worth looking at, and many of them would help you form the solid nucleus of a personal advertising and marketing library.

Before I sign off and leave you to explore the lists in this book, let me address a nagging issue. While most of the business world greeted the original *Words That Sell* with enthusiasm and gratitude, a few critics from ad agencies have sniped at its "color-by-numbers" approach to what is, for them, an art form. They claim that such books promote clichés and otherwise uninspired copy. These critics have a point, but they miss the larger one.

If you work for a boutique ad agency that prizes image and edginess over bottom-line effectiveness, my *Words That Sell* books probably aren't for you. But if you need proven words and phrases that actually motivate customers to *buy*, the color-by-numbers argument becomes irrelevant. It's always nice to win advertising awards (and I've won my share), but it's even more satisfying to see your words get results.

Like its predecessor, *More Words That Sell* does not pretend to be exhaustive. In the coming months and years, you'll run across plenty of words and phrases that would have made first-rate entries. When you do, just jot them down under the appropriate heading and expand the collection. After all, I want my book to become *your* book.

BUSINESS-TO-BUSINESS ADVERTISING

Are you in the business of doing business with other businesses? If so, always remember that you're still in the business of reaching *individual people*—the people behind those desks who read your advertising and decide whether to order your products and services. You're not talking to an institution, so your language shouldn't sound institutional. Professional, yes—but also warm and inviting.

Keep in mind that recipients of business advertising are motivated by most of the same drives as ordinary consumers: they have wants, needs, and fears just like anyone else. They want to succeed. They want their *organization* to succeed. They need to be respected by their colleagues. They fear being left behind. They dread failure. In short, they're you and me.

This list begins with a basic business advertising vocabulary and then supplies you with a collection of phrases that I've found to be especially effective.

business	providers
company	suppliers
organization	employees
solution	management
tool	clients
training	customers
product	prospects
program	professional
application	cost-effective
partnership	high-performance
strategy	productive

productivity
targeted
marketing
on-site
budget
sales
revenue
profit
bottom line
sell-through
competition
free consultation
your business
Make critical decisions.
Make smarter business decisions.
Build your business.
Grow your business.
Get your sales rolling.
Make your business prosper.
Turn your business around.
Now any size company can . . .
Provide —— like a multimillion-dollar business.
Let —— put your business on top of the competition.
Stay one step ahead of the competition.
Gain an unfair advantage over your competition.
If you want the edge over the competition, we're the answer.
All successful ——s have one thing in common.
Create professional-looking ——.
The select few who have seen this —— are begging for access.

This information is not available anywhere else.
Get in on the action.
Successfully market any product, service, or opportunity.
Now it's easier than ever to launch and promote your ——.
Get your message to the right prospects.
Build your database.
Access millions of leads.
Send a powerful message to your customers.
Maintain customer satisfaction at all levels of interaction.
Seal the deal.
We want to be your —— expert.
We supply all the materials you need to start.
Buy direct from the source.
We're on call wherever you go, whenever you need us.
Retrieve your —— whenever you need it.
We created the —— so you don't have to.
Learn what works and what doesn't.
Our system eliminates ——.
Save time and money.
Reduce —— costs.
Trying to cut expenses?
Are you paying too much for ——?
at a fraction of the cost
Let's talk about how much you can save.
Stretch your ad budget.

Focus your budget on your
    business essentials.
Unlock your profit potential.
See the results start to materialize
    within weeks.
These same techniques have
    generated . . .
I'll show you how others are
    succeeding.
I'll answer your every question.
If you're tired of hype, . . .
Our packages start as low as
    $——.
Get your free estimate.
Forward this message to your
    coworkers NOW.
sets a new standard
empowers your employees
brings you closer to your
    customers
streamlines your logistics
does __% of the work for you
boosting our clients' bottom lines
keeps your bottom line healthy
ensures a great return on your
    advertising dollar
gives your company the agility it
    needs
expert-led
professional consultants with
    proven track records
the market leader in . . .

provider of . . .
a dynamic, affordable —— tool
best solution for your needs
total solution
solutions you can extend to
    customers and employees alike
high-performance tools
more productive ways to . . .
for your customers, partners, and
    stakeholders
improved work flow
bullet-proof security
unlimited sales leads
top-rated tools from ——
easy to use
clear and easy to understand
minimal learning curve
with minimal training
self-paced training solutions
beyond the basics
without breaking the bank
with no up-front investment
free setup
no set-up costs
low start-up costs
low operating costs
no support costs
no monthly fees
Take our —— for a free test-drive.

For further inspiration, see:
Online Marketing Services

CEREBRAL WORDS

Some words appeal to the head rather than the heart or the gut. Most of the words on this extensive list are derived from Latin, and they still project an unmistakable whiff of respectability.

I've restricted the list to vocabulary that a businessperson or professional might use, so you won't stumble across intellectual gems like *otiose* or *objurgate* here. Perhaps in a future book.

Use these words to fortify your résumé, business correspondence, in-house reports, and other documents that demand a tone of maturity and competence. If you're not sure of a word's meaning, be sure to look it up. Impressive words badly used can subvert the professional image you're trying to create.

The list is arranged alphabetically. You can scan it for five-dollar words to incorporate into your business writing. Or use it as a glossary (without definitions, of course) for the purpose of building a solid working vocabulary.

A word of warning: Don't become too intimate with these words; they're respectable but not especially lovable. Treat them as colleagues who can help you in the workplace. Then go home for the day and relax with unpretentious old friends like *swift*, *swipe*, and *shuffle*.

Note: *Don't* make a point of using these words in your advertising copy. In fact, you might want to go out of your way to avoid most of them. This list is primarily for professional image building.

ability	accomplish
abstract	account
access	accurate
accommodate	acknowledge

acquire	balanced
adapt	basis
adequate	benefit
adjust	bias
administer	capital
adopt	certainty
advantage	circulate
adverse	classified
advise	coherent
affiliation	collaborate
affirmative	commitment
affluent	communicate
aggressive	competence
align	competitive
alliance	comprehend
allocate	compromise
alternative	concept
ambiguous	conclusive
amendment	conditional
analogy	conducive
analyze	conduct
anticipate	conjecture
application	conscientious
appraise	consequence
appropriate	consider
arbitrary	consistent
articulate	consolidate
assessment	consult
assimilate	contend
associate	continuous
assumption	control
assurance	conventional
astute	conversant
attribute	conversely
authorize	cooperate
autonomous	correlation
auxiliary	corroborate

counsel

data

decision

decline

define

delegate

demographic

demonstrate

dependent

derive

determine

dictate

differentiate

direction

disadvantage

discern

discharge

disclose

discrepancy

discretion

discriminate

disseminate

disservice

distinctive

distribute

diverse

documentation

dominate

educate

effective

efficacy

efficient

elect

element

entitle

envision

erroneous

essential

estimate

evaluate

examine

expedite

facilitate

fact

fallacy

favorable

fidelity

finite

fiscal

flexibility

fluctuate

focus

forecast

formulate

fulfill

function

fundamental

futile

generate

generic

global

govern

graduated

gravitate

guarantee

guidance

hesitate

hypothesis

ideal

identity

ignorance

imagination

impatient

impeccable

impede
impersonal
implement
inability
incidental
incisive
inclination
inclusive
incompatible
inconsistent
indefinite
index
indispensable
inevitable
infer
influence
information
inhibit
initiate
innovate
input
insist
inspect
institute
instruction
instrumental
insure
integral
integrate
intelligent
intent
interaction
interfere
intermediate
internal
interpret
intersect

intrinsic
intuitive
invaluable
inventory
investigate
involve
issue
judgment
judicious
justify
legacy
legislate
legitimate
leverage
liability
limitation
literal
logical
lucid
magnitude
management
manifest
marginal
mastery
maximize
mediate
medium
mentor
merit
metaphor
method
meticulous
minimize
misguided
mission
mobility
model

moderate
modify
module
monitor
motivate
multiple
mutual
nebulous
necessity
negative
negotiate
network
neutral
noncommittal
objection
objective
obligation
obscure
observe
obsolete
obstruct
obtain
obvious
omission
operation
opinion
opposition
option
orderly
organization
orientation
original
outline
paradigm
paradox
parameter
participate

particular
partnership
patronize
pattern
penalty
penetrate
perception
performance
peripheral
permanent
permutation
perpetuate
persevere
persistent
perspective
persuade
pertain
phase
plan
plausible
position
positive
possibilities
potential
practical
pragmatic
precarious
precaution
precipitate
precision
preclude
preconceived
predict
predominantly
preference
preliminary
premature

premise	punitive
premium	pursue
preparation	qualified
prerogative	quality
prescription	quantity
presentation	questionable
preserve	quota
prestige	radical
presume	random
pretext	rate
prevail	ratio
prevent	rational
primary	reaction
principal	realize
principle	reasonable
priority	reception
proactive	reciprocal
probable	recognition
proceed	recommend
process	record
produce	recoup
professional	recover
proficient	redefine
prognosis	reduction
program	reference
progress	refine
prohibit	reflect
project	refute
promote	regard
proportion	regulation
propose	rehabilitate
prospect	reimburse
prosper	reinforce
protect	reject
prototype	relative
provide	release
provisional	relevant

reliable
relinquish
reluctant
remainder
remote
render
reorganize
reply
report
represent
reputable
requirement
research
resemble
residual
resist
resolve
resource
respect
response
responsibility
restore
restrain
restrict
results
retain
revert
revise
rhetoric
rigorous
routine
sanction
scenario
schedule
scrupulous
scrutinize
segment

select
seniority
sensible
sequential
service
singular
skill
solicit
solution
specific
speculate
stability
standard
statement
statistic
status
stimulate
stipulate
strategy
structure
study
subjective
submit
subordinate
subscribe
subsequent
subsidize
substantial
substitute
subvert
success
successive
succinct
suggest
summary
superficial
superfluous

superior
supersede
supervise
supplement
surpass
suspect
suspend
sustain
symptomatic
synopsis
synthetic
system
tactics
tangential
technology
temperament
tendency
tenuous
terminate
testify
theory
traditional
transaction
transcend
transfer
transform
transient
transition
translate
transpose
ultimate
unacceptable
unconditional
undermine
understand
understated
unequivocal

unfit
unit
universal
unlikely
unquestionable
unreasonable
unsound
urgent
useful
utilize
vacillate
validity
value
vanguard
vehicle
venture
verbal
verify
versatile
viability
vindicate
violate
virtual
visibility
vision
vocation
volume
voluntary
wisdom
withdraw
yield
zone

For further inspiration, see:
**Classified Ads: Employment;
Negative Qualities; Personal
Qualities**

CLASSIFIED ADS: EMPLOYMENT

Need to hire some qualified help for your growing company? Maybe it's time to write a want ad. You can place an ad in your local paper, in trade magazines, on your website, or on some of the more popular job market sites.

You'll want to say a few words about your organization; the nature of the job; the professional qualifications you expect; the personal traits you'd like the applicant to possess; your relaxed (or high-pressure) work environment; the salary level (at least a hint); and, of course, how you'd like the applicant to contact you. The trick is to pack all that information into a space the size of an address label.

I've assembled some of the most effective words and phrases used by human resources departments. When you write your ad, put yourself in the shoes of the potential applicants and see if you'd be motivated to respond. Tweak the ad copy until the job sounds like an offer you (and *they*) can't refuse!

Make your mark.
Prestigious —— company seeks . . .
Leading —— company seeks . . .
Growing —— company seeks . . .
Progressive —— company seeks . . .
—— invites you to . . .
internationally recognized leader in ——
challenging position
high-profile position
front-line position

great résumé builder
tremendous opportunity
unique advancement opportunity
excellent growth opportunity
opportunity to apply your talents
a stable and rewarding career
entry-level position
immediate opening
immediate F/T position
Primary responsibilities include . . .

Duties include . . .
Qualified candidate will have . . .
Ideal candidate has . . .
Must be able to . . .
Must have . . .
. . . a must.
Proven —— skills a must.
Desire to excel essential.
—— degree required.
Solid background in —— required.
—— required, —— a plus.
Background in —— preferred.
minimum —— years experience
—— experience required.
expert knowledge of ——
broad knowledge of ——
expertise in ——
top-notch portfolio
strong interpersonal skills
excellent verbal and written
    communication skills
excellent computer skills
excellent management skills
proven leadership skills
good organizational and team-
    building skills
strong skills and smarts
Understand all aspects of . . .
Must be able to meet demands
    of . . .
plan and develop
build
supervise
implement
oversee
run
lead

Provide strategic leadership . . .
Interface with top management.
Work closely with . . .
Work well under pressure.
If you are committed to . . .
If you want a career instead of a
    job . . .
If you have the right mix of
    skills . . .
energetic
high-energy
dynamic
assertive
highly motivated
financially motivated
resourceful
articulate
well-spoken
highly intelligent
smart
smarts
business smarts
biz sense
bright
savvy
talented
skilled
proficient in ——
qualified
eye for detail
competent
hardworking
task-oriented
multitasking
organized
effective
efficient

punctual
self-motivated
self-starter
can-do attitude
take-charge individual
team player
people-oriented
enthusiastic
outgoing
friendly
ethical
outstanding compensation
great earnings
top pay
excellent salary and benefits
excellent growth and earnings
    potential
competitive salary
competitive benefits package
annual bonus based on
    performance
stimulating environment
exciting environment
fast-paced environment
deadline-oriented environment
high-pressure environment
dynamic team environment
friendly environment
stable, congenial environment
low-pressure environment
casual environment
fun atmosphere

flexible hours
Be your own boss.
beautiful facilities
will train
Submit cover letter and résumé
    with salary requirements to . . .
E-mail your résumé to . . .
Include salary
    history/requirements.

Some Handy Space-Saving Abbreviations

background—bkgd
environment—envt
excellent—exc
experience—exp
immediate—immed
intelligent—intel
knowledge—knowl
management—mgmt
minimum—min
opportunity—oppty
organization/organizational—
    org
professional—prof
qualified—qual
requirements—req
salary—sal
years—yrs

For further inspiration, see:
Personal Qualities

CLASSIFIED ADS: MERCHANDISE

Brevity is the soul of a classified ad. Eliminate every single word that doesn't help sell your item. Good-bye to articles like *the* and *an*! Go back and cut the longer words down to size wherever possible. (The newspaper staff will often perform that task for you, but ask in advance just to make sure.) The final ad should be as tight as possible but still easily understood.

This list is primarily for sellers of used merchandise (including vehicles), where the universal concerns are condition and price. (You'll find that most of the phrases gravitate around those two topics.)

If you're selling your own brand-new products in a classified format, there really are no special response-boosting words or phrases that you need to know—other than the universal response-boosting words and phrases that apply to all advertising. You simply want to catch the reader's attention and make the sale in a minimum of space. The trick is to keep it brief without sacrificing color, interest, or essential information.

Factory-fresh.	Looks like new.
Never opened.	Superb cond(ition).
Never used.	Runs great.
Mint cond(ition).	Works great.
New cond(ition).	Looks and handles great.
Perfect cond(ition).	Great shape.
Flawless cond(ition).	No scratches.
Runs perfect.	No dents.
Like new.	Used —— times.
Almost new.	Hardly used.

Lightly used.
Meticulously maint(ained).
Well maint(ained).
Fine cond(ition).
Good cond(ition).
Used cond(ition).
Needs TLC.
Needs some work.
Needs work.
Sold as is.
Completely rebuilt.
Very collectible.
Prof(essional) quality.
Heavy-duty ——.
Good for college or new
   ap(artmen)t.
Stores flat.
Orig(inal) box.
Orig(inal) owner.
With all orig(inal) parts.
Loaded.
Many extras.
Photo avail(able).
E-mail photo avail(able).
Call for details.
Call after —— p.m.

Call for price.
Flexible price.
Price negotiable.
All offers considered.
Est(imated) value $——.
Best offer.
Best offer over $——.
Asking $——.
Book price $——, asking
   $——.
Was asking $——, now $——.
$—— firm.
Financing avail(able).
Deliv(ery) avail(able).
Will swap.
You pick up.
Serious inquiries only.
Liquidation sale!
Must sell!
Moving—must sell!
Must see!
Nice!
Great value!

For further inspiration, see:
Magic-Response Words

CLASSIFIED ADS: PERSONALS

What's this? A section on *personal ads* in a Serious Advertising Thesaurus? Absolutely. Who says advertising has to be all business? The fact is, some of the most effective short ads are written by people speaking passionately on behalf of themselves, in search of kindred spirits and elusive chemistry.

If you're unattached and unafraid of personal ads, turn to this section to describe yourself and the person of your dreams. I've omitted all the specialized interests (jazz, bird-watching, long walks on the beach, etc.) that tend to fill such ads. (You can fill in the blanks yourself.) But you'll find a smorgasbord of desirable human traits to choose from. Happy hunting!

Both Sexes

appealing
attractive
presentable
decent-looking
good-looking
great-looking
head-turning
cute
cuddly
lovable
huggable
sexy
sensuous
slim
lean
medium build
well-proportioned
well-built
plus-size
fit
athletic
outdoorsy
active
youthful
healthy
health-conscious
fun to be with

funny	versatile
whimsical	interesting
silly	intriguing
humorous	open-minded
great sense of humor	enlightened
great personality	spiritual
charming	soulful
spontaneous	ethereal
mischievous	introspective
flirtatious	sensitive
romantic	refined
passionate	patrician
fiery	preppy
energetic	classy
outgoing	upscale
friendly	sophisticated
gregarious	intelligent
confident	bright
streetwise	articulate
adventurous	witty
well-traveled	book-lover
cosmopolitan	cultured
urbane	educated
worldly	successful
independent	hardworking
nonconformist	goal-oriented
liberal values	professional
irreverent	financially secure
sassy	sensible
frisky	down-to-earth
playful	unpretentious
free spirit	uncomplicated
funky	old-fashioned
cool	conservative values
eclectic	family-oriented
well-rounded	religious
multitalented	respectful

polite
considerate
caring
easy to talk to
good listener
sympathetic
empathetic
compassionate
loving
affectionate
sweet
gentle
kind
good-hearted
decent
honest
outspoken
frank
no-nonsense
sincere
reliable
dependable
faithful
commitment-minded
stable
marriage-minded
mature
thoughtful
serious-minded
emotionally secure
positive
born optimist
upbeat
easygoing
laid-back
mellow
neat

fresh-scrubbed
well-groomed
impeccable
elegant
glamorous
Looking for . . .
like-minded
soul mate
best friend
kindred spirit
the right person
blissful monogamy
partner for life
no baggage
no games
companionship
friendship first
friendship—possibly
    more
Looking to build a life
    with . . .
age/race/religion/looks
    unimportant

Women Only

winsome
adorable
alluring
pretty
lovely
beautiful
bewitching
radiant
ravishing
drop-dead gorgeous
stunner
exotic

luscious
petite
svelte
willowy
shapely
curvaceous
voluptuous
statuesque
full-figured
feminine
natural beauty
sprite
temptress
goddess
vivacious
saucy
charmer
lady

Men Only

handsome
ruggedly handsome
trim
muscular
burly
husky
heavyset
dapper
debonair
dashing
rakish
rugged
masculine
all man
stud muffin

teddy bear
gentleman

Some Handy Space-Saving Abbreviations (in typical order of appearance)

1. Marital status/orientation

divorced—D
gay/lesbian—G
single—S
widowed—WW

2. Race/ethnicity (optional)

Asian—A
black/African-American—B
Hispanic—H
white—W

3. Religious (optional)

Christian—C
Jewish—J

4. Gender

female—F
male—M

Other (mention in body of ad)

nondrinker—N/D
nonsmoker—N/S
long-term relationship—LTR

For further inspiration, see:
Personal Qualities

CLASSIFIED ADS: REAL ESTATE

Most real estate ads are written by real estate professionals. But if you have a property to sell and you want to bypass the middleperson, you'll have to write your own ad.

I don't have to tell you that real estate is very expensive and real estate ads are very brief. That means each word in your ad bears a colossal sales burden. You have to write a tight ad that manages to cover the essential details and convey the pleasure of owning the property. Most newspaper staffs will help you to shorten your ad through tactical abbreviations of longer words, but check in advance to see if they do.

Sounds like a tough challenge, doesn't it? The good news is that you don't have to close the sale through your ad. You merely have to entice your readers to come out and visit the property (without creating unrealistic expectations). Then it's up to you to close the sale in person.

By the way, if you happen to be a real estate professional, feel free to crib from this list!

Location, location, location!

Great buy!

Live in style!

Live large!

Country living!

Comfort and intimacy!

Penthouse luxury!

Awaiting your arrival.

Hilltop views!

Your home in the sky!

Serious buyers only!

Must see!

Must sell!

Available immediately!

Move right in!

Don't miss out!

Hurry!

Get it before it's gone!

stately	Antebellum
majestic	Victorian
dramatic	Tudor
classic	Colonial
elegant	Art Deco
stunning	prewar
gorgeous	modern
romantic	contemporary
storybook	farmhouse
deluxe	carriage house
sophisticated	bungalow
timeless elegance	row home
spacious	twin
supersize	ranch
oversized ———	split-level
palatial	bi-level
luxurious detail	period details
architectural details	lots of character
handcrafted detail	great potential
exquisite details	fab potential
lots of built-ins	needs your TLC
fully appointed	handyman
all appliances	great starter
amenities galore	restored
great layout	fully renovated
curb appeal	lovingly renovated
vintage	recently remodeled
historic landmark	freshly painted
historic gem	airy
charming	bright
cute	sun-filled
cozy	glorious light
intimate	soothing light
period charm	shady
Old World charm	quiet
pre-Revolutionary	tranquil
Federal	pristine

mint

immaculate

new construction

brand-new

architect-designed

one-of-a-kind

custom-built

unique

elevator building

doorman building

coveted building

prestigious building

full-service building

chef's kitchen

eat-in kitchen

Overlooks . . .

panoramic views

breathtaking views

lush country estate setting

professionally landscaped

secluded retreat

country charm

pastoral

safe

secure

peaceful

lovely grounds

parklike setting

privately gated

cul-de-sac

tree-lined street

great block

quiet street

quiet neighborhood

secluded neighborhood

vibrant neighborhood

prestigious neighborhood

up-and-coming neighborhood

prime area

walking distance to ——

Walk to ——.

——-minute walk from ——

—— minutes from ——

near shopping and
    transportation

convenient location

ideally located

centrally located

easy commute

Asking $——.

price negotiable

price on request

well priced

Max home, mini price!

Some Handy Space-Saving Abbreviations

bathrooms—bths (or ba)

bedrooms—BR (or bdrms)

building—bldg

cathedral ceiling—cath ceil

central air conditioning—cent A/C
    (or CAC)

dining room—DR

duplex—dplx

extra large—x-lg

family room—fam rm

finished basement—fin bsmt

fireplace(s)—fplc

furnished—furn

garage—gar

hardwood floors—hdwd flrs

in-ground pool—in-grd pl

Jacuzzi—jacuz

MORE WORDS THAT SELL

kitchen—kit

laundry room—lndry rm

living room—LR

location/located—loc

private—pvt

renovated—renov

screened porch—scrn pch

service—svc

skylights—skylts

view—vu

COLORS

The world glows with a dazzling array of hues that no crayon box could possibly contain, and we've given them an equally dazzling array of names. This list was a joy to compile, and it's one of the few in this book that you can turn to for sheer pleasure on a rainy day. (Try "Flavors," "Fragrances," and "Sexy Words," too.)

If you're in the business of marketing products in various colors, use this list when you need to give those colors appropriate and appealing names. Color names can be direct or subtly evocative, classic or playful. Be sure to choose a name that fits the image of your product. (For example, you probably wouldn't want to market *Wedgwood blue* to kids or include *bubblegum pink* in a catalog of upscale men's wear.)

This section begins with a list of prefixes that you can use to modify your color names. Then we run the gamut of colors through the spectrum from reds to purples, followed by earth tones, neutrals, and metallic hues.

Common Prefixes

pale
dusty
faded
light
medium
bright
dark
deep
deepest
raw
burnt
warm
hot
cool
ice
true
pure

solid
fluorescent
antique
mellow
vintage
heritage
colonial
French
British
Chinese
burnished
polished
glossy
satin
matte
flat

Red

wine
port wine
burgundy
bordeaux
claret
merlot
sangria
beetroot
maroon
crimson
deep rose
cinnabar
rhubarb
pomegranate
apple red
candy apple
black cherry
wild cherry
cherry

berry
raspberry
raspberry sorbet
cranberry
strawberry
holly berry
garnet
ruby
cardinal red
poppy
geranium
scarlet
lipstick red
gumdrop red
fire-engine red
hot pepper
pimiento
true red
radical red
rocket red
regal red
ravishing red
razzle-dazzle red
vintage red
Pompeii red
barn red
rouge
russet
redwood
bacon
brick
tile red
terra cotta
rust
cinnamon
paprika
cayenne

hot spice
carnelian
Martian red

Orange

vermilion
auburn
copper
burnished copper
antique copper
salmon
henna
robin's breast
burnt orange
flame
fireball
molten lava
oriole orange
firebird orange
neon orange
fluorescent orange
outrageous orange
organic orange
awesome orange
flaming orange
orange crush
carrot
tangerine
clementine
persimmon
mango
papaya
pumpkin
cheddar
sweet potato
cantaloupe
nectarine

peach
pale peach
peaches 'n' cream
creamsicle
kumquat
apricot
apricot brandy
amber

Yellow

ginger
saffron
curry
honey
butterscotch
gold ochre
mustard
buff
sand
straw
jute
tawny
flaxen
blond
topaz
wheat
buckwheat
frankincense
champagne
chardonnay
maize
corn silk
pale yellow
sunflower
sunburst
sunrise yellow
sunshine

sun devil
solar yellow
yummy yellow
yahoo yellow
fluorescent yellow
mellow yellow
vintage yellow
dandelion
daffodil
marigold
buttercup
lemon peel
lemonade
lemon sherbet
quince
pineapple
ripe banana
deep yellow
canary
finch yellow
goldenrod
golden
gold
antique gold
ancient gold
burnished gold
mellow gold
old gold
pale gold
sun gold
antique brass
burnished brass

Green

chartreuse
celadon
celery

yellow-green
pale green
spring green
lime
lime sherbet
limeade
kiwi
mint green
mint leaf
sage
dill
basil
oregano
pistachio
surf spray
sea foam green
sea grass
honeydew
apple green
asparagus
avocado
olive
deep olive
loden
juniper
willow
eucalyptus
moss
chaparral
cactus
ivy
fern
shamrock
meadow grass
grass green
herb green
alpine green

kelly green
Irish green
parrot green
bottle green
vintage green
antique green
leaf green
woodland green
forest green
black forest
hunter green
evergreen
pine
hemlock
balsam
spruce
dark fir
royal palm
alpine green
tropical green
neon green
fluorescent green
goblin green
ghoulish green
glorious green
chlorophyll
emerald
tourmaline
jade
malachite
verdigris
copper green
blue-green

Blue

teal
robin's egg blue

baby blue
aquamarine
turquoise
Persian blue
peacock blue
ice blue
blue haze
powder blue
slate blue
steel blue
marlin blue
Prussian blue
Wedgwood blue
china blue
Federal blue
Union blue
cornflower
morning glory
hydrangea
chicory blue
sky blue
azure
cyan
blue flame
neon blue
fluorescent blue
blazing blue
seafarer blue
sea blue
maritime blue
ocean blue
Mediterranean blue
Aegean blue
Caribbean blue
Atlantic blue
Pacific blue
Baltic blue

Arctic blue
Neptune blue
cerulean
celestial blue
cobalt
royal blue
French blue
British blue
Dutch blue
lapis lazuli
sapphire
blueberry
true blue
vintage blue
blue denim
blue heaven
blue lagoon
blue funk
dark blue
deep blue
ultramarine
navy
midnight blue
ink blue
indigo
blue-violet

Purple

pale purple
periwinkle
lavender
lilac
wisteria
orchid
hyacinth
iris
violet

petunia
grape
concord grape
glorious grape
grape jelly
aubergine
eggplant
blackberry
deep purple
plum
pixie dust
amethyst
purple passion
purple twilight
royal purple
deep wine
mulberry
boysenberry
thistle
mauve

Pink

pale rose
antique rose
dusty rose
rose quartz
rose petal
rosebud
carnation
magenta
fuchsia
cerise
deep pink
berry
watermelon
bubblegum pink
cotton candy

pink lemonade
pink champagne
strawberries 'n' cream
teaberry
hot pink
neon pink
electric pink
fluorescent pink
shocking pink
tickled pink
strike me pink
pretty in pink
whisper pink
pale pink
powder pink
blush
nude pink
cherub pink
baby pink
flamingo
coral
shrimp
salmon

Brown

mahogany
cherry wood
sequoia
chestnut
walnut
maple
oak
acorn
cork
sandalwood
hazel
pecan

hickory
nut brown
nutmeg
brandy
cognac
whiskey
cola
toffee
caramel
molasses
gingerbread
light toast
warm toast
toasty brown
brown sugar
sepia
bronze
antique bronze
burnished bronze
ancient bronze
cappuccino
latte
café au lait
mocha
coffee
cocoa
chocolate
double fudge
espresso
umber
burnt sienna
earth brown
fawn
camel
saddle
log cabin
brownstone

vintage brown
deep brown

Tan/Beige

taupe
suntan
deep tan
tropical tan
desert tan
canyon tan
camouflage
fatigue
olive drab
khaki
desert khaki
field khaki
British khaki
vintage khaki
peanut shell
sesame
rattan
rope
burlap
natural linen
moccasin
suede
buff
ochre
chamois
palomino
dune
sand
desert sand
sandy tan
sandstorm
warm sand

sandblast
sandstone
pueblo tan
hacienda tan
adobe
stucco
ecru
neutral
driftwood
barley
rye
bisque
cream of wheat
oatmeal
porridge
mushroom
almond
Swiss almond
macadamia
meringue
stone
soapstone

White

parchment
canvas
ivory
antique ivory
bone
oyster
cream
buttermilk
milk white
mayonnaise
eggshell
vanilla

antique white
Navajo white
lemon ice
coconut
chalk white
swan's down
dove white
plume white
titanium white
true white
whitewash
birch bark
sailcloth
lace
cotton puff
edelweiss
moonglow
pale moonlight
starlight
milky way
frost
snowflake
snowfall
snowball
snowdrift
winter white
glacier white
Arctic white
polar white
ghostly white
whiter-than-
    white
bright white
steam
pearl
platinum

Gray

grey
steel gray
iron gray
ash
smoke
smokestack
smoky quartz
smoky gray
stone gray
slate
flagstone
fieldstone
cobblestone
granite
pumice
putty
clay
dove gray
pigeon gray
warm gray
thundercloud
thunderhead
thunderstorm
tornado
stormy gray
elephant gray
gray flannel
Confederate
    gray
cadet gray
French gray
blue-gray
pearl gray
Tahitian pearl
silver gray

silver cloud
silver
antique silver
ancient silver
pewter
gunmetal
graphite
charcoal gray

Black

ebony
raisin
blackberry
peppercorn
raven
licorice
noir
blue-black
india ink
lamp black
midnight black
night sky
deep space
obsidian
onyx
anthracite
coal black
coal dust
charcoal
jet black
tuxedo black
basic black
Goth black
black diamond
blackout

fade-to-black
blackest black
blacker-than-black
extreme black
boldest black

Metallic

golden
gold
antique gold
ancient gold
burnished gold
mellow gold
old gold
pale gold
sun gold
antique brass
ancient brass
burnished brass
polished brass
copper
burnished copper
antique copper
bronze
antique bronze
burnished bronze
ancient bronze
silver gray
silver
antique silver
ancient silver
pewter
gunmetal
platinum
titanium

EMOTIONAL WORDS

Emotion is the soul of advertising. You want your words to rouse your readers from indifference and propel them to action. The words in this section will help you break through the indifference barrier. They're packed with varying degrees of emotional voltage.

The first few lists are full of positive emotional words. Then we descend into what looks like a pit of darkness and despair. Don't shy away from negative words like *pain*, *heartache*, and *shame*. They're powerful motivators for people who want to avoid grief in their lives—and who doesn't?

You'll find the negative words especially useful if you're trying to tug at the heartstrings of prospective charity donors. They'll help you paint a vivid picture of the dire conditions your organization is trying to correct.

Affection

feel
care
caring
sympathy
empathy
compassion
tenderness
fondness
like
love
loving
passion

enthusiasm
zest
mad about
rapture
ardent
fervor
smitten
bewitched
adorable
sweet
cute
lovely
dear

endearing
cherish

Cheer

happy
delighted
thrilled
enchanted
roused
excited
overjoyed
rejoicing
jubilant
elated
exhilarated
exuberant
glad
cheerful
giddy
merry
wild
insane
loopy
high
soaring
tingling
tickle
laugh
laughter
giggle
snicker
glee
mirth
joy
joyous
enjoy
gaiety

play
playful
romp
fun
sunny
sizzling
hot
warm
heartwarming

Thriving

belong
soothe
soothing
comfort
comforting
contentment
serene
secure
pride
power
strength
strong
flourishing
blossoming
triumphant
radiant
vibrant
vivacious
lively
lucky
fortunate

Hope

hopeful
believe
belief

faith
wish
aspire
desire
yearn
ache
dream
heartening
eager
upbeat

Anguish

bleak
stark
dire
cold
dismal
gloomy
forlorn
lonely
depressed
unfortunate
trapped
frustrated
smothered
overwhelmed
helpless
hurt
abused
wretched
miserable
misery
agony
distress
poverty
pain
grief

grieving
mournful
heartache
heartbreak
shock
scream
cry
sob
weep
sorrow
pity

Failure/Shame

cheap
inferior
worst
tacky
shameful
ashamed
bungling
stumble
washout
fiasco
loss
loser
beaten
degraded
rejected
outcast
humbled
demoralized
demeaning
humiliating
humiliation
disgrace
ruined
crushed

Fear

worry
anxiety
fright
panic
jitter
chilling
numbing
scare
dread
horror
horrifying
terror
terrifying
hell
hellish

Anger/Cruelty

mad
upset
sour
bitter
offended
resentment
jealousy
envy
greed
ferocious
fierce
savage
vicious
angry
seething
fuming
bristling
disgusted

hate
hatred
wrath
rage
fury
furious

Violence

shatter
smash
wreck
wreckage
destroy
destruction
awful
wanton
cruel
brutal
horrendous
terrible
evil
ghastly
torture
rape
kill
death
slaughter
murder
butchery
bloodshed
massacre
genocide

For further inspiration, see:
**Negative Qualities; Nonprofit
Fundraising; Verbs**

FINANCIAL ADVERTISING

Opportunity, convenience, privilege, and trust—those are the four cornerstones of financial advertising. First you appeal to the nearly universal desire to save or make money—ideally accompanied by visions of the wonderful things your reader can do with that money. Then stress how easy it is to do business with your organization—and how the reader will enjoy VIP treatment after opening an account. Finally, back up your promises with the assurance that your company is as sound as the Federal Reserve. (If your product or service involves financial risk, always be up-front about it.)

Whether you're advertising a lending service, a credit card, a stock brokerage firm, or a financial seminar, you can use this list to pepper your ad with response-getting phrases. The list begins with key words I've culled from the financial advertising that has found its way into my mailbox, then moves on to more elaborate phrases.

Note: Sorry, you won't find any phrases here for multilevel marketing schemes. If you're about to follow that career path, all I can say is, "Turn back!"

finances	rate
investment	account
savings	performance
money	return
cash	gain
portfolio	profit
budget	risk
bills	access
credit	preferred

preapproved
solid
sound
strategies
opportunity
debt-free
financial freedom
financial independence
financial stability
financial flexibility
financially savvy
instant money
fast cash
generous credit line
a powerful financial tool
a highly flexible financial
    partner
profit potential
create wealth
immediate cash flow
cash back
great low rates
zero liability
no annual fee
no interest on —— until ——
grace period
You know a good deal when
    you see one.
one of the best deals around
the advantages you demand
flex your budget
protect your credit
simplify your bookkeeping
maximize your savings
share the privileges
Consolidate your bills today!
Cut your taxes in half!

Put some extra money in your
    pocket.
See and interpret trends . . .
If you can stomach some risk, . . .
Give away less and keep more.
Manage your finances with ease
    by . . .
Track your account activity day or
    night.
secure online account management
smarter investment approach
in an unpredictable financial
    climate
Should you be worried?
. . . will help protect you and your
    family.
If the unexpected should
    happen, . . .
boosts your purchasing power
your investment priorities
your line of credit
low introductory rate
the lowest rate we've ever offered
Be debt-free in weeks . . .
You've earned the privilege . . .
You've already earned this
    opportunity.
You're already preapproved.
You're automatically covered . . .
Because of your status, . . .
your superior credit record
your superior standing
You are among a select group . . .
As a preferred customer, . . .
exclusive savings unavailable to the
    general public
We're happy to reward you . . .

Use this money any way you want.

Access your money whenever you want.

money that's available when you need it

Imagine putting in $—— on Monday and having $—— on Friday!

a stunning return of ——%

Don't miss your chance to get in early!

a smart way to maximize your savings

Save as much as $—— a day!

Start saving money today.

saves you money every time you use it

The savings can last year after year.

Save for your dream vacation, a second home, your child's college education.

The sooner you reply, the sooner you start saving.

The sooner you reply, the sooner you start making money.

Would you like to be financially independent?

Gain the financial independence you've always dreamed about.

They're beginning to learn my secret.

Discover a hidden marketplace . . .

We've collected some of the best financial advice . . .

We help you avoid the pitfalls of . . .

simple money-making strategies

winning strategies

the secrets of today's most successful money managers

secrets your stockbroker won't tell you

what your broker won't tell you

a solid financial strategy

solid fundamentals

an essential financial resource

solutions to your biggest financial dilemmas

a wealth of opportunity

It's reassuring to know . . .

peace of mind

sound operating performance

You can count on ——'s rock-solid reputation and service.

If you ever need help with your account, we're just a toll-free phone call away.

Call —— to discuss your options.

For further inspiration, see:
Personal/Professional Growth

FLAVORS

Caution: Don't spend too much time with the following list! Reading it from top to bottom could cause you to ransack the nearest cupboard and pack on some serious weight.

But this list has its uses. If you need to describe a food product, enhance a menu, or think of new flavors to add to your product line, this is the place to visit. The idea is to make the reader's mouth water.

The list begins with general flavor-related words and phrases, then moves on to specific flavors, most of them evocative and yummy. *Bon appétit!*

taste	hearty
flavoring	juicy
flavorful	succulent
flavorsome	salty
delectable	salted
delicious	briny
luscious	spicy
yummy	spiced
epicurean	herbal
ambrosial	herbed
appetizing	minty
tantalizing	peppery
mouthwatering	peppered
savory	curried
tasty	hot
zesty	red-hot

nutty	tender
mellow	fluffy
sharp	chewy
tangy	crisp
tart	crispy
sour	crackly
fruity	glazed
fresh	toasty
lemony	toasted
sugary	roasted
sugared	seared
sweet	grilled
sweetened	barbecued
honey-sweet	smoked
honeyed	cured
bittersweet	broiled
bitter	browned
chocolaty	baked
fudgy	poached
buttery	fried
buttered	stir-fried
creamy	panfried
creamed	deep-fried
full-bodied	blackened
ripe	flambéed
dense	sizzling
rich	stewed
decadently rich	steamed
sinfully rich	steaming
killer ——	boiled
death by ——	boiling
whipped	simmering
light	done to perfection
light as air	a taste of . . .
delicate	laced with . . .
subtle	sprinkled with . . .
lean	bursting with . . .

a medley of . . .
a hint of . . .
a pinch of . . .
flavored with . . .

A list of flavors

vanilla
vanilla bean
cocoa
chocolate
chocolate chip
chocolate chunk
white chocolate
milk chocolate
bittersweet chocolate
dark chocolate
fudge
fudge swirl
double fudge
marshmallow
s'mores
graham cracker
rocky road
butterscotch
caramel
molasses
brown sugar
cane sugar
maple sugar
maple syrup
honey
peanut butter
peanut
almond
toasted almond
hazelnut
chestnut

walnut
pecan
praline
date
fig
raspberry
blackberry
strawberry
blueberry
cranberry
elderberry
gooseberry
lingonberry
mulberry
huckleberry
grape
concord grape
raisin
currant
black currant
cherry
black cherry
wild cherry
sour cherry
peach
nectarine
apricot
plum
prune
pear
apple
candy apple
green apple
orange
tangerine
clementine
lemon

lime
key lime
grapefruit
melon
cantaloupe
honeydew
watermelon
mango
papaya
pineapple
banana
coconut
guava
passion fruit
kiwi
cola
ginger
mustard
Dijon mustard
honey Dijon
horseradish
wasabi
horehound
licorice
anise
caraway
nigella
sesame
tahini
coffee
café au lait
latte
cappuccino
espresso
mocha
caffe mocha
chai

green tea
mint
cool mint
peppermint
spearmint
wintergreen
teaberry
cinnamon
nutmeg
cloves
paprika
chili
curry
pepper
peppercorn
red pepper
cayenne pepper
salt
sea salt
rock salt
cumin
oregano
basil
tarragon
rosemary
sage
thyme
coriander
dill
cilantro
parsley
chives
scallion
onion
Vidalia onion
garlic
olive

caper

pimiento

tomato

beet

eggplant

pumpkin

zucchini

celery

cucumber

pickle

relish

salsa

guacamole

avocado

corn

potato

sweet potato

wheat

semolina

oat

rice

barley

soy

lentil

mushroom

portobello mushroom

anchovy

shrimp

crab

Chesapeake blue
   crab

Alaska king crab

Dungeness crab

lobster

tuna

yellowfin tuna

salmon

Atlantic salmon

Pacific salmon

chicken

roast chicken

barbecued chicken

southern-fried chicken

turkey

duck

Peking duck

pâté

liver

beef

roast beef

London broil

hamburger

steak

filet mignon

meatball

veal

lamb

pork

ham

Smithfield ham

Black Forest ham

bacon

Canadian bacon

sausage

chorizo

andouille

bratwurst

knockwurst

kielbasa

salami

pepperoni

pizza

fresh pasta

oil

olive oil
vinegar
wine vinegar
balsamic vinegar
mayonnaise
egg
milk
buttermilk
yogurt
sour cream
cream
butter
cheese
cheddar
Gruyère
Swiss cheese
Jarlsberg
bleu cheese
Roquefort
Stilton
Gorgonzola
feta
Brie
Camembert
nacho cheese
Monterey jack
mozzarella
provolone

Romano
Parmesan
ricotta
cream cheese
cheesecake
sponge cake
devil's food
brownie
gingerbread
meringue
fruitcake
rum
tequila
margarita
whiskey
bourbon
brandy
cognac
sherry
port
wine
beer
ale
stout

For further inspiration, see:
Fragrances

FRAGRANCES

Words are miraculous in their ability to evoke sensations. Think about it: you're looking at a series of black squiggles on a white background. But when you see a phrase like *wood smoke* in print, your brain can trick you into experiencing the memory of a chilly autumn day in your childhood.

Words that evoke fragrances have the power to rouse our senses (and make us more receptive to the message). You don't even have to be selling perfume or food products to harness this power.

This list begins with generic "smell words" and phrases that are descriptive in nature. The second part of the list bombards you with examples of distinctive fragrances you can use to make your copy more sensually evocative. I've only scratched the surface. When you have a free moment or two, you might want to jot down your own favorite smells.

smell	fresh
scent	fruity
scented	minty
aroma	spicy
aromatic	musky
fragrance	mossy
fragrant	woody
perfumed	smoky
balmy	incense
flowery	sea breeze
floral	ocean breeze
herbal	bracing

pungent
acrid
spring garden
summer garden
seaside garden
English garden
woodland scent
smells that transport you back to
    your childhood
the wonderful aromas of your
    grandmother's kitchen
zesty aroma
sharp aroma
bold aroma
tantalizing aroma
enticing aroma
captivating aroma
intoxicating aroma
heady aroma
heavenly aroma
evocative aroma
the ravishing scent of a woman's
    perfume
a faint trail of perfume
the earthy scent of leather
a whiff of ——
a breath of ——

the scent of . . .

lilacs
hyacinths
roses
rosewater
honeysuckle
honey
jasmine
orange blossoms

oranges
lemons
fresh citrus
apples in the fall
sliced peaches
mint leaves
tomatoes fresh off the vine
allspice
cloves
cinnamon
nutmeg
basil
oregano
rosemary
sage
parsley
cilantro
peppermint
cinnamon
vanilla
chocolate
hot chocolate
toasted almonds
fresh-roasted peanuts
buttered popcorn
bacon
barbecue
French fries
French bread
fresh-baked bread
fresh-baked cookies
pizza baking in the oven
an old-time bakery
soup on the stove
herbal tea
coffee in the morning
freshly shampooed hair

fresh laundry
a baby in a blanket
puppies
a wet dog
a spring day
balsam
northern hemlocks
cedar
pine
wood smoke
hickory smoke

burning leaves
a garden in the rain
mossy woods
musk
incense
burning candles
beeswax
crayons

For further inspiration, see:
Flavors

HEALTH AND FITNESS

People who feel sick want to feel well. That much is obvious. But over the past few decades we've come to expect more from our mortal bodies: people who already feel well want to feel even better. They want to live to be a hundred and go to their final reward looking fifty. Baby boomers, especially, tend to be obsessed with their own well-being (I'm one of them), and they're getting older every day.

If you have a legitimate product or service that promotes "wellness," you have a huge market ready to grab your offer. That's the good news. The bad news is that you have at least two major hurdles to overcome: an abundance of competition and an almost equal abundance of public skepticism regarding instant cures.

Since half of any cure is in the mind, you'll want your advertising to convey how it *feels* to feel well—strong, vibrant, confident, and renewed. Once your prospects can visualize their own good health, you (and they) are halfway there. The other half is assuring your audience that you can deliver on your promises.

Feel free to use gentle scare tactics (the dangers of a sedentary life, the specter of an early demise or an infirm old age) to motivate your readers to respond. But don't let the negative outweigh the positive; introduce your product or service as the proverbial white knight. Make liberal use of testimonials (especially from recognized experts) to lend extra credibility to your message.

relieve	recover
release	restore
relax	rebound
revive	reinvent
renew	reinvigorate

rejuvenate
look great
get strong
boost your metabolism
burn fat
slim down
your ideal weight
without yo-yo dieting
a diet that's as sensible as it is
    effective
Watch those excess pounds melt
    away.
Shed those unsightly extra
    pounds!
Lose —— lbs. in —— days—
    guaranteed!
guaranteed weight loss
firms your ——
replace flab with muscle
build muscle
add muscle bulk
bulk up
cut your cholesterol
lower your blood pressure
ignite your sex drive
improve your sex life
rejuvenate your love life
enhance your sexual satisfaction
boost your sexual performance
boost your energy level
banish pain
freedom from pain
restore flexibility
enjoy deeper, more restful sleep
wake up refreshed
relaxation exercises
deep relaxation

improve your memory and
    alertness
keep your sanity
eliminates wrinkles
banish ——
fast relief from ——
promotes rapid healing
live longer
live better
feel better
feel younger
youth-enhancing
Slow down and even reverse the
    effects of aging.
Beat stress in —— minutes.
stress management
chronic stress
harmful effects of stress
ease tension
wellness
coping tips
Tests have shown that . . .
clinically proven
proven approach
positive approach
mind-body connection
Important medical breakthrough!
our team of scientists
Learn the art of ——.
Take control of your ——.
You can do it.
—— ways to ——
Win compliments . . .
Health is more than the absence of
    disease.
works with your body's own
    healing process

provides the nutrients your body
  needs
natural remedy
all-natural
ultrapotent
It's not a pill.
easy tablet form
FDA-approved
safe and effective
no side effects
promotes a healthy ——
bodywork
lifestyle changes
therapy
program

support groups
aerobic exercise
massage
meditation
guided imagery
aromatherapy
yoga
self-hypnosis
powerful antioxidants
organic
herbal
pure

For further inspiration, see:
Personal/Professional Growth

MAGIC-RESPONSE WORDS

I f I had to sift through this book and pick out a single list for you to memorize, this would be it. (Of course, since you have the book, you can simply flip to this page.) You're looking at the timeless words and phrases that have always "worked like magic" to win customers and probably always will. As long as customers are human, these words won't go out of style.

Notice that the words on this list appeal directly to the reader's elemental needs: a bargain, a fleeting opportunity, the urge to belong, the urge to *possess*, the pursuit of happiness, and the avoidance of pain. Professional copywriters (especially *direct-marketing* copywriters, whose success depends on measurable results) have been using these words for decades to convert prospects into customers and keep customers coming back for more. Pay close attention to this list and use it often.

free	offer
save	special offer
savings	exclusive offer
discount	limited-time offer
bargain	clearance
$—— off!	closeout
——% off!	Everything must go!
sale	markdown
gift	value
free gift	money-saving
special	economical
bonus	pays for itself

now	unique
right now	genuine
tips	proven
tricks	tested
secrets	safe
answers	secure
facts	no-nonsense
fast	practical
instantly	successful
. . . in minutes	professional
good	powerful
better	amazing
best	like magic
best-rated	smart
top-rated	famous
big	acclaimed
biggest	important
more	essential
most	valuable
unlimited	total
extra	complete
less	all-inclusive
easy	includes everything you need
simple	Here's what you get:
no-fuss	here's how
low-maintenance	plus
handy	you
convenient	we
new	I
improved	win
fresh	discover
latest	learn
up-to-the-minute	look at . . .
innovative	compare
breakthrough	create
revolutionary	boost
original	build

enhance	never
collect	always
get	forever
take	hurry
make	today
earn	for a limited time only
enjoy	act now
deserve	don't wait
succeed	don't miss
call	urgent
act	opportunity
join	visit us
avoid	call for details
end	click here
save	order
shop	send for
stop	send no money
go	free trial
works	risk-free
helps	no risk
solves	no obligation
delivers	free shipping
performs	guarantee
at last	satisfaction guaranteed
finally	completely
for the first time	owe nothing
the first	only $——
the only	will you
Only —— gives you . . .	please
only from ——	thank you
just for you	yes
exclusive	as seen on TV

NEGATIVE QUALITIES

Most advertising and promotional writing accentuates the positive. That's understandable. But don't overlook the power of negative words and feelings. These emotionally loaded words and phrases trigger basic human instincts (like fear, anger, or sympathy) that can drive a response in your favor.

How do you use negativity to sell? Well, you can always badmouth the competition (politicians have been doing it for ages). Without naming names, you can contrast the shoddiness of similar products with the virtues of your own. I've provided a bundle of words and phrases for that purpose. But there are more sophisticated strategies for using negativity in advertising. The key is to set up a nightmare scenario that the reader dreads: financial hardship, ill health, cockroaches in the kitchen sink. Then you point to your product or organization as the white knight charging to the rescue.

Sift through this compilation of wretchedness and inferiority whenever you want to harness the unique power of negativity to get your message across. I've clumped the words into alphabetically arranged categories for easy reference.

Confusing

baffling	difficult
blurred	elaborate
unclear	convoluted
bewildering	impenetrable
mind-boggling	perplexing
complicated	puzzling
	mixed up

ambiguous
vague
hazy
obscure
nebulous
a maze of . . .

Dull

drab
boring
dreary
flat
arid
dry
uninteresting
pedestrian
prosaic
uninspired
lackluster
unimaginative
colorless
lifeless
wooden
humdrum
sterile
tedious
monotonous
tiresome
wearisome
ponderous
stuffy
starchy
a yawn
puts you in a stupor
sleep-inducing
stagnant

sluggish
slow

Fake

phony
bogus
copy
replica
clone
imitation
artificial
simulated
counterfeit
poor substitute
fabrication
sham
mock-——
pseudo-——
would-be
wannabe
imitator
impostor
pretender
charlatan
quack
pale imitation of . . .

Inferior

badly made
cheap
shoddy
flimsy
poor
lesser
unsteady
shaky

wobbly
rickety
weak
fragile
feeble
unsound
defective
substandard
mediocre
low-grade
worthless
no-name
minor-league
second-quality
second-rate
third-rate
rejects
the pits
dregs
bottom of the
  barrel

Miserable

sick
ill
unhealthy
tired
weary
exhausted
drained
worn out
unhappy
sad
gloomy
dismal
joyless

depressed
dejected
downcast
despondent
despairing
luckless
wretched
desolate
lonely
forlorn
isolated
abandoned
humiliated
degraded
squalid
sordid
nasty
tawdry
poor
needy
destitute
impoverished
poverty-stricken
unfortunate
misfortunes
setbacks
adversity
distress
agony
grief
pain
anguish
heartache
heartbreak
hopelessness
give up hope

Pretentious

snooty
snobbish
elitist
affected
precious
sanctimonious
snide
smirky
sniffy
vain
ostentatious
showy
arty
extravagant
arrogant
judgmental
persnickety
lofty
pompous
bloated
puffed-up
uptown
gentrified
yuppified
self-important
self-proclaimed
soi-disant (self-proclaimed)

Rigid

hard
harsh
strict
tough
stern
severe

stiff
mechanical
exacting
unbending
inflexible
stubborn
knee-jerk
backward
stilted
wooden
starchy
proper
priggish
puritanical

Ruined

dilapidated
damaged
tainted
contaminated
run-down
destroyed
wrecked
reduced to ruins
broken
shattered
demolished
state of collapse
pulverized
smashed
dashed
trashed
crushed
undone
subdued
overwhelmed

overcome
eliminated
finished
irreparable
history
left in the dust
beyond hope

Scary

startling
alarming
frightening
awful
terrible
terrifying
horrifying
horrific
horrendous
chilling
hair-raising
bloodcurdling
macabre
ghoulish
fiendish
diabolical
evil
dreadful
ghastly
frightful
fearsome
grotesque
appalling

Shallow

superficial
skin-deep

one-dimensional
just skims the surface
lightweight
frivolous
glib
slick
slippery
commercial
mindless
insipid
inane
vapid
pointless
bleating
dumb
petty

Too Little

insufficient
deficient
inadequate
skimpy
meager
scrawny
puny
measly
insubstantial
lightweight
thin
diluted
watered down
shriveled
shrunken
faded
worn out
burned out

gone dry
underwhelming
poverty
shortage
deficiency
deficit
need
deprivation

Too Much

excessive
wasteful
spendthrift
extravagant
extreme
glut
surplus
unwieldy
hulking
lumbering
laden with . . .
heavy
bulky
added bulk
cumbersome
chubby
bulging
fat
a profusion of . . .
a deluge of . . .
a plethora of . . .
cloying
over-the-top
overwhelming
overpowering
smothering

Unappealing

unappetizing
uninviting
ungracious
uncivilized
tasteless
crude
ugly
unsightly
smelly
foul
slimy
greasy
oily
rancid
stale
bitter
sour
tainted with . . .
sloppy
dirty
filthy
soiled
littered with . . .
messy
shabby
dingy
unsanitary
unsavory
unbecoming
unflattering
unattractive
disagreeable
unpleasant
obnoxious
offensive

obscene
gross
lousy
crummy
tacky
tawdry
trashy
nasty
repulsive
revolting
loathsome
disgusting
sickening

Unreliable

unsound
unsafe
untested
questionable
impractical
suspicious
risky
chancy
dangerous
untrustworthy
disreputable
dishonest
wily
tricky
shifty-eyed
unprincipled
unfit
unqualified
unprofessional
incompetent
inept

amateurish
careless
indifferent
disorganized
inconsistent
haphazard
uneven
Don't fall for . . .

Unsuitable

unwarranted
improper
unfitting
undue
incongruous
inappropriate
unnecessary
unnatural
strange
weird
bizarre
a bad fit
a square peg
mismatch

Wrong

false
inaccurate
incorrect
mistaken
erroneous
untrue
untruthful
unproven
unsubstantiated
unjust

unfair
inflated claims
distorted
skewed
wrongheaded
misguided

faulty
a bad choice

*For further inspiration,
see:* **Emotional Words;
Verbs**

NONPROFIT FUNDRAISING

You're looking at one of the most difficult and rewarding forms of advertising. Your prospects have already been bombarded with countless pleas from other worthy organizations, so you have to make your own plea stand out from the crowd. On top of that, you have no concrete benefits to offer—just the warm ripple of satisfaction that comes from making a small but positive difference in the world. That's your ball, and you have to run with it.

You have an arsenal of strategies at your disposal. Start with a bleak picture of conditions as they are (or have been in the past), then portray your organization as the unique bridge between despair and hope, disaster and relief. Always stress the urgency of the situation. Praise your readers for their concern and generosity. Emphasize how little you're really asking of them in terms of time and money. Remind them how much their small contribution can help—whether they're coming to the aid of impoverished children or endangered grizzly bears. And be sure to let them know how *good* it feels to help.

This isn't crass manipulation. If you believe in the mission of your organization, it's the simple truth.

gift	commitment
contribution	fight
generosity	challenge
support	efforts
caring	critical
concerned	vital
children	urgent
mission	ongoing

plea
implore
you
we
us
together
raise
help
save
rescue
join
member
A catastrophic —— is
    unfolding . . .
Our —— is at stake.
We could lose —— forever, and
    that would be an unimaginable
    tragedy.
As many as —— people are at
    risk . . .
in desperate straits
As always, the children suffer
    most.
Not everyone is so lucky.
Today we have an opportunity
    to . . .
It's not too late for us to save
    ——.
It takes just a few cents a day . . .
It's up to you . . .
You have the ability—and the
    responsibility—to . . .
You can make the difference
It's up to those of us who care
    about ——.
It's up to us to act.
I implore you . . .

If you share my belief, . . .
Please do your part to . . .
You can play a key role . . .
your active involvement
your financial support
your vitally needed support
We need your support and we need
    it now.
We need your immediate action.
your swift response
There's no time to waste.
before time runs out
people who care enough to give
care deeply about . . .
concerned people like you
Please accept this —— as our
    "thank you" for your
    generosity.
Please continue reading.
If you don't do it for yourself, do it
    for . . .
With your generous gift . . .
the power of your gift
Please join us in our fight.
Together, we can . . .
We can take on the —— and win.
I urge you to join forces with us
    now.
Join a select group of
    individuals . . .
Join us in standing up to . . .
Help us raise the amount we need
    to . . .
Add an important voice . . .
Generate a groundswell of public
    opinion.
Here's what's at stake:

a long list of challenges

critical issues

critical efforts

urgent action

Make sure they get the message.

Make your voice heard.

We've won a major victory.

We work locally with communities, businesses, and concerned people like you.

We'll be undertaking major initiatives.

an outspoken advocate for . . .

We're deeply committed to . . .

We will win the battle to . . .

our ongoing struggle to . . .

to carry on our mission

recommit ourselves to the great challenges facing us . . .

We're not out to save the world, just its ——.

If we don't act now to save ——, who will?

Think how much we stand to gain—and how little it costs you.

Give what you can today.

Your membership support will enable us to . . .

Thank you for your generous past support.

Your membership renewal will help us carry on our vital work.

With your continued support, . . .

your ongoing support

your ongoing commitment to . . .

If you keep giving, we'll keep fighting . . .

Please consider increasing your level of support.

Please take a moment right now, while you still have this letter in your hand, to . . .

Just fill out the enclosed membership form and return it in the mail today.

Ask your company if it will match your contribution.

special members-only benefits

For further inspiration, see:
Emotional Words

ONLINE MARKETING SERVICES

Probably half the unsolicited E-mail that enters my in-box is from purveyors of online marketing services. No matter how much of a battering the tech sector might take (and we all know it has taken plenty), Web commerce is here to stay. Nearly every business or organization needs its own site to stay viable. Nearly every site needs expert help from professionals who can design it, optimize it, and reach customers through E-mail advertising.

When you promote online marketing services, remember that you're creating business-to-business advertising first and foremost. Emphasize what you can do for the bottom line of your potential client and how you go about doing it. It's fine to impress your audience with a handful of high-tech buzzwords, but the three most important words to keep in mind are *traffic, traffic, traffic*! Always subordinate the tech details to the main message of generating greater revenue for your client.

This list starts with a brief catalog of basic Internet vocabulary to keep in mind as you write. Then it continues with the most effective phrases I've culled from all those E-mail messages that have reached my desktop. I've even concocted a few of my own.

online	search engine
navigate	ranking
download	site
upload	link
broadband	hits
streaming	visits
pixels	unique visitors
cookies	page views

traffic

banner

pop-up

opt-in

click

click-through

E-mail

subscribe

unsubscribe

webmaster

FREE download!

Click here to download your free ——.

Download your free trial version.

Drive qualified traffic to your site.

Ensure that online shoppers find you.

Reach the greatest number of potential clients.

There are millions of potential buyers out there for nearly anything you want to sell.

the power of word-of-mouth referrals

Bring those visitors back for more!

Keep your customers coming back.

Not making enough from your site?

Raise your site ranking FREE!

optimization strategies

Boost your traffic by 10, 100, or even 1,000 times!

grows your traffic

a steady stream of new visitors

links that get you clicks

your online source

top ten ways to . . .

search engine visibility

search ranking

opt-in E-mail system

real-time ——

Just —— cents per click!

with just a few clicks

See results start to materialize in as little as —— days!

Make your living online!

Make money surfing the Web!

the exact step-by-step methods that an Internet millionaire uses daily to rake in $——

home-based business opportunity

lucrative online niche

residual income stream

Now it's easier than ever to launch and promote your own ——.

viral marketing

guerrilla marketing

without spamming

You can succeed on the Internet right now.

the power of E-mail marketing

Use direct E-mail to turn your business around.

Track your own advertising.

. . . does ——% of the work for you!

top-rated Web tools

incredible tool for webmasters

the most versatile —— on the market

award-winning software

automatic referrals

user-friendly (overused)

secure and reliable
the Net's foremost ——
E-commerce
You won't have to worry about
    lost connections.
Hit the ground running.
superior ease of use
simple navigation
for ease of navigation
not for geeks only
keep document weight down
load quickly
Which of these mistakes are you
    making with your Internet
    marketing?
Deliver the information your
    visitors want.
Right from your desktop!
Plug into the world's best ——
    system.

any time of day or night
works for you while you sleep
Showcase your ——.
It's only an E-mail away.
It's only a click away.
We respect your online privacy.
To unsubscribe, simply click the
    link at the bottom of this
    message.
Click here if you prefer not to
    receive E-mail from ——.

For further inspiration, see:
**Business-to-Business
Advertising; Technology
Advertising; Web Copy;
Appendix D: Online
Copy**

PERSONAL/ PROFESSIONAL GROWTH

The self-improvement movement may have peaked in the late twentieth century, but people will always feel a need to improve their lot. That means they're already receptive to your proposition, at least in theory.

Whether you're trying to sell a book, a seminar, or a personal organizer, what you need to remember (and remind your readers of) is (1) that so few of us are using our potential, (2) that it *feels absolutely wonderful* to achieve things we didn't know we could achieve, and (3) that your program or product can help us achieve them. Always keep your tone warm and positive.

To help people become their best selves is one of the nobler callings in the world of marketing. I've supplied you with a list of commonly used words and phrases that ripple with the thrill of self-empowerment. Use them freely, but be creative as well. Try to combine some of these words into exciting new patterns. Better yet, see if you can come up with the next great self-improvement catchphrase—a fitting heir to *Your Erroneous Zones* or *7 Habits of Highly Effective People.*

growth	possibilities
change	potential
challenge	knowledge
life	education
spirit	success
dream	successful
positive	harmony
productive	balance
productivity	balanced

centered

achieve

achievement

transform

transformation

create

creation

creativity

wake up

fulfill

fulfillment

enrich

enrichment

enhance

enhancement

life-enhancing

abundance

self-esteem

self-confidence

insights

solutions

secrets of success

subliminal

Tap into the . . .

Harness the power of your

    ———.

Attract ——— into your life.

limitless opportunities

new opportunities for . . .

Recapture your . . .

Let go of . . .

programs your subconscious

your blueprint for achievement

strategies for taking charge of

    your life (career)

Take the first step toward a more

    rewarding life (career).

Take a lesson from the superstars

    of . . .

Dare to dream!

Dare to become the success you

    were meant to be.

Create more time to do what you

    love to do.

will change your life

the challenge of change

fostering positive change

arms you with vital insights

Pick up vital new skills . . .

new competitive skills

Stay competitive . . .

Fine-tune your ____ skills.

Broaden your knowledge base.

Arm yourself with vital

    information . . .

Don't get left behind . . .

Work smarter, not harder.

. . . both on and off the job

Achieve more in less time.

Create winning habits . . .

Act more effectively . . .

helps you and your organization

    forge ahead

Turn your dreams into

    achievements.

If you can dream it, you can

    achieve it!

Make your vision a reality.

Turn fear into confidence.

Turn your unproductive hours into

    time well spent.

Turn your free time into learning

    time.

Invest in your future.

Make a small investment in
  yourself.
a small investment that will repay
  itself many times over
personal coaching
personalized training
your training needs
flexible training option
training initiatives
train-the-trainer program
We teach people to teach
  themselves.
Our skilled trainers empower your
  people to succeed.

Achieve your organizational
  goals.
We deliver —— to your
  workplace.
customized for your organization
group exercises
interactive discussions
. . . at the personal, interpersonal,
  managerial, and organizational
  levels

For further inspiration, see:
**Emotional Words; Health and
Fitness**

PERSONAL QUALITIES

The lion's share of this book is designed to help you promote your products and services. This section will help you promote *yourself*—along with friends, colleagues, interns, students, or anyone else whose success matters to you.

I've collected the most positive-sounding personal qualities and grouped them into ten major categories for easy reference. These are the traits employers and college admissions officials look for when they evaluate applicants. Use these lists whenever you need to compose a dynamic cover letter, update your résumé, fill out an application, write a letter of recommendation, or run for office.

Of course, you won't always want to use glowing terms to describe other people, especially if you're a politician or a journalist. If you feel the need to sling mud, just turn to the "Negative Qualities" section.

Able/Effective

capable
proficient
competent
highly competent
top-notch
talented
gifted
a master of . . .
first-rate
skilled
skillful
organized
efficient
productive
enterprising
industrious
hard-driving
hardworking
persevering
thorough
proactive
responsive
adaptable

flexible
resourceful
responsible
reliable
dependable
punctual
alert
serious
judicious
motivated
competitive
powerful
successful
respected
esteemed
born leader
problem solver
solution-driven
resolves issues
peak performer
high-performance
committed to . . .
handles conflict
exceeds expectations
passionate about winning

Attractive

good-looking
great-looking
super-looking
fine-looking
fit-looking
impressive
charismatic
magnetic
engaging
youthful

graceful
patrician
elegant
neat
impeccable
well-groomed
appealing
fetching
winsome
enticing
alluring
charming
bewitching
captivating
radiant
glowing
luminous
gorgeous
head-turning
pretty
lovely
cute
feminine
ethereal
svelte
willowy
statuesque
streamlined
slim
trim
lean
muscular
well-built
handsome
dapper
dashing
rakish

virile
rugged
boyish

Bold/Energetic

gutsy
passionate
impassioned
ardent
outspoken
vocal
sassy
irreverent
provocative
independent
principled
courageous
fearless
fierce
audacious
adventurous
venturesome
daring
valiant
gallant
intrepid
dynamic
a dynamo
a pistol
a whirlwind of energy
vibrant
vital
amazing vitality
high-energy
proactive
assertive
competitive

aggressive
hard-driving
fast-moving
forceful
commanding
powerful
a powerful presence
magnetic
charismatic
strong
vigorous
enterprising
innovative
progressive
farsighted
single-minded
freewheeling
gonzo
wild-and-crazy
a maverick
a born leader
sees the big picture
embraces change
welcomes new challenges
challenges the status quo
willing to take chances
takes calculated risks
knows when to take risks
pursues opportunities
mover-and-shaker
keeps things moving

Creative

original
individual
independent
inner-directed

perceptive
spiritual
farsighted
visionary
inspired
imaginative
spontaneous
playful
stimulating
talented
gifted
prodigious
ingenious
inventive
interesting
offbeat
intriguing
exotic
unconventional
incomparable
singular
unique
one of a kind
sui generis (one of a kind)
a rare one
novel
fresh
refreshing
single-minded
probing
bold
provocative
innovative
productive
prolific
resourceful
impassioned

passionate
artistic
an artist
a genius (don't overuse)
Renaissance man/woman
a master of . . .
thinks outside the box

Decent

good-natured
completely trustworthy
thoroughly reliable
of the highest character
rock-solid character
highest standards of conduct
of the highest integrity
unimpeachable
ethical
principled
highly principled
right-minded
moral
moral fiber
morally sound
straight arrow
gallant
upright
upstanding
honest
truthful
honorable
incorruptible
virtuous
kind
considerate
polite
refined

civilized
well-mannered
gentle
sensitive
cooperative
accommodating
unselfish
selfless
unselfish
compassionate
caring
traditional
unpretentious

Experienced

qualified
eminently qualified
highly qualified
seasoned
dedicated
skilled
skillful
accomplished
veteran
judicious
proficient
professional
adept
authoritative
distinguished
well-versed
expert
expertise
years of expertise
expert knowledge of ——
—— years' experience
——-year veteran

a distinguished career
a long and productive career
a long career devoted to . . .
know-how
sound judgment
proven track record
proven —— skills
proven ability
solid background
extensive background
distinguished background
award-winning
has won numerous accolades
respected by his/her peers
a recognized authority
a seasoned pro
been around the block
understands all aspects of ——
the résumé says it all

Friendly/Outgoing

enthusiastic
energetic
lively
vivacious
vibrant
charismatic
magnetic
dynamic
spirited
sunny
effervescent
exuberant
upbeat
cheerful
playful
spontaneous

engaging
fun
funny
whimsical
merry
earthy
open
honest
frank
sincere
amiable
likable
lovable
affectionate
genial
congenial
sociable
extroverted
people-oriented
cordial
courteous
gracious
generous
appreciative
good-natured
easygoing
pleasant
well-liked
winning personality
easy to work with
an ideal colleague
gets along with everyone
a "people person"
a good listener
gives off good energy
gives off good vibes
someone you'd want to work with

Intelligent

smart
gifted
talented
skilled
highly skilled
highly intelligent
brilliant
astute
bright
sharp
savvy
a quick study
quick-thinking
alert
keen
acute
analytical
incisive
adroit
deft
adept
shrewd
clever
witty
articulate
well-spoken
sophisticated
literate
learned
educated
scholarly
intellectual
knowledgeable
civilized
worldly
logical

rational
sensible
thoughtful
perceptive
insightful
ingenious
probing
resourceful
stimulating
top-notch
—— smarts
street-smart
an elegant mind
a first-rate mind
a dazzling intellect

Reliable

steady
stable
sane
sober
serious
sensible
no-nonsense
level-headed
reasonable
rational
dedicated
diligent
thorough
punctual
prompt
efficient
careful
deliberate
detail-oriented
prudent

scrupulous
judicious
dependable
trustworthy
trusted
professional
businesslike
rock-solid
unflappable
poised
calm
cool-headed
even-tempered
sound
healthy
fit
decent
confident
secure
emotionally secure
grounded
centered
honest
direct
candid
straightforward
unpretentious
down-home
earthy
traditional
gifted with common sense
a high degree of
    professionalism
a team player
supports team efforts
"can-do" attitude
never misses a ——

performs under pressure
comes through in the crunch

Versatile

adaptable
adjusts easily
flexible
able to wear many hats
a quick study
talented
multitalented
multidimensional
well-rounded
rare combination of talents
Renaissance man/woman

broad background
worldly
bilingual
multilingual
jack-of-all-trades
valuable utility player
knows all aspects of . . .
well-versed
familiar with all areas of the
   business

For further inspiration, see:
Classified Ads: Employment;
Classified Ads: Personals;
Negative Qualities

PHYSICAL WORDS

Some of us have to unlearn what we learned in college. (That's one of the ironies of writing effective advertising copy.) Don't worry—I'm not asking you to forget about political science, art history, or other worthy subjects. Instead, you should try to reduce your reliance on the kind of abstract language you picked up as you were writing all those term papers.

This section should help you rediscover the power of earthy, tactile words—the kind of words that bleed if you cut them. Think of Churchill's "blood, toil, tears, and sweat." These physical words summon up visceral responses in the reader's mind. They help make your message more immediate, more alive, more likely to break through the reader's indifference barrier.

bare	willowy
naked	wispy
nude	elastic
shapely	flexible
ripe	lithe
thick	lean
plump	long and lean
dense	streamlined
full-bodied	sinewy
fleshy	muscular
contoured	hot
clean lines	steamy
light	simmering
airy	boiling

sizzling	gush
scorching	spray
burning	spritz
smoldering	snap
balmy	pop
cool	glide
chilled	slide
cold	shuffle
frozen	bounce
icy	rock
misty	flutter
foamy	tumble
creamy	stumble
smooth	flap
polished	jostle
speckled	flurry
flecked	flip
sprinkled	dodge
peppered	drag
stippled	tug
dappled	chug
mottled	creep
glossy	crumple
shiny	crumble
bright	swagger
glowing	plod
luminous	slither
radiant	trudge
lustrous	trample
translucent	lunge
dark	lurch
deep	slug
abyss	slam
erupt	spin
explode	skid
blast	crash
burst	sprawl

prowl
twitch
itch
squirm
shiver
shudder
swoop
swoosh
swipe
wag
whoosh
wiggle
wrestle
toil
crank
pump
drill
press
pull
hoist
lift
heft
heave
toss
fling
jettison
dump
scrap
hack
cut
clip
lop
slice
snip
split
slash
rip

peel
grate
grind
squash
squish
squeeze
smear
soak
scrub
scour
scratch
claw
scrape
shred
whittle
chop
churn
gulp
gobble
guzzle
lick
smack
slurp
hiccup
sneeze
sniff
grin
scowl
frown
blush
stretch
bend
squat
thrust
crouch
crawl
blood

tears
sweat
shower
cleanse
powder
dust
soot
dirt
mud
muck

earth
water
air
fire

For further inspiration, see:
**Flavors; Fragrances;
Negative Qualities; Plain
Words; Sexy Words; Sounds;
Textures; Verbs**

PLAIN WORDS

Sometimes you just want to chuck the whole pretentious yuppified world we live in and return to something simpler. More honest. Less edgy and ironic. Less Seinfeld and more Jimmy Stewart.

If your product or service appeals to our primal need for simple goodness, you should be using good, simple words. The kind of words Lincoln or Will Rogers would have used. Even if you're trying to promote technology or upscale fashions, it wouldn't hurt to visit this list and reacquaint yourself with the unvarnished power of plain words. They feel good, and they'll make your readers feel even better.

plain	wholesome
truth	fresh
pride	pure
trust	real
honor	natural
honest	wild
decent	free
good	rugged
better	tough
best	rough
fine	solid
not bad	strong
rare	weak
common	soft
simple	quiet

smooth
light
fair
dark
deep
hot
warm
cool
cold
sharp
mild
dull
new
old
wise
foolish
silly
funny
brave
bold
stop
go
start
sweet
sour
wet
dry
slow
fast
poor
cheap
broken
made
hewn
handmade
homemade

homegrown
home
family
life
live
alive
fit
care
friend
neighbor
peace
calm
ease
easy
hard
work
play
enjoy
like
love
fond
need
want
help
feel
know
dream
get
give
take
plenty
things
stuff

For further inspiration, see:
Emotional Words; Physical Words

SENIOR MARKET

Today's old people were yesterday's young people. You shouldn't feel the need to treat them as relics. They want to enjoy life as much as anyone. And now that retirement has liberated them from the daily grind, they actually have the time to indulge their desires. Only two factors might prevent them from doing so: their health and their finances. No wonder these two concerns loom so large in most advertising for the senior market.

Put yourself in the shoes of your senior audience before you craft your message. Old age isn't for sissies. Your readers face a limited and uncertain future, but most of them are gritty survivors and they're not ready to roll over. They just want assurance that you can make life easier for them in some small way.

Note the special concerns of the senior market: staying healthy, active, and connected; enjoying the security of a steady income; finding a good bargain; avoiding scams that could drain their resources; discovering new interests to keep their minds alive; remembering the old days with tenderness; enjoying vacations, hobbies, socializing, and time with their families; and preparing for the eventual shift to assisted living.

Treat old people kindly and fairly. Their generation nurtured ours, after all, and someday we'll be in their shoes.

seniors	elements of a healthy lifestyle
older citizens	live longer
older Americans (Canadians, etc.)	antiaging
retirees	stopping the aging process
your retirement years	the right prescription
retirement havens	staying healthy and active

senior singles
caregiving support
assisted living
long-term care
keeping Alzheimer's at bay
keeping busy
mentoring
tutoring
volunteering
making a difference in your
    community
age discrimination
coping with grief
finding new friends
caring for yourself
caring for your loved ones
caring for your precious heirlooms
a new career
your dream vacation
time for your grandchildren
enjoy reminiscing . . .
the golden age of ——
when they still knew how to write
    songs
a nostalgic look at ——
Relive favorite moments from . . .
words of comfort and faith
Be safe, not sorry.
Are you getting the most for your
    money?

Avoid —— rip-offs.
Outsmart scam artists.
affordable
hot deals
senior discount
for the savvy consumer
on a fixed income
on a limited income
residual income
stream of income
annuity
home-based business
an ideal business for your
    retirement
older investors
Plan for your future.
Avoid financial hardship.
your retirement nest egg
your Social Security
    benefits
your supplemental Medicare
    options
fiscal fitness
Rebuild your finances.
starting over
It's never too late.

For further inspiration, see:
**Financial Advertising; Health
and Fitness**

SEXY WORDS

et's face it: sex sells. Generations of successful advertisers have enticed us with images that light our inner fires. You can do it with pictures (too easy, I say) or you can do it with words alone.

I've shaped this list to include the obvious (*nude* and *sinful*, for example) as well as more subtly suggestive words (e.g., *whisper*, *blush*, and *rustle*) that I think are even sexier. The right words, especially those with the right sounds and mental associations, can work magic on the page—and in the minds of your readers.

Note: You don't have to be writing about sex (or even sexy products) to use sexy words. You could be describing fruit baskets or office products. The key is to use the scintillating verbal imagery of sex to stimulate lust for your products.

naked	feline
nude	lean
bare	firm
ripe	hard
supple	hard-bodied
soft	sinewy
flowing	brawny
swaying	fleshy
musky	luscious
earthy	tender
lithe	moist
sleek	liquid
slinky	dewy

creamy

smooth

silky

velvety

satiny

downy

sheer

see-through

diaphanous

revealing

womanly

feminine

ultrafeminine

female

waiflike

elfin

androgynous

male

manly

masculine

macho

magnetic

alluring

bewitching

flirtatious

coy

demure

discreet

modest

delicate

intimate

scintillating

head-turning

saucy

sassy

daring

shameless

suggestive

immodest

scandalous

sinful

naughty

decadent

passionate

forbidden

raw

lust

kiss

caress

touch

tickle

rub

massage

feel

blush

tingle

throb

glow

ache

desire

pleasure

rapture

ecstasy

ear lobes

nape

shoulders

breast

waist

hips

curves

buns

derriere

thigh

panties

undies
stockings
nylons
lingerie
camisole
slip
negligee
bikini
briefs
robe
sheets
bedroom
night
moonlight
cool
whisper
shadows
rustle

hush
sigh
gossip
innuendo
tango
samba
tropics
hot
warm
steamy
sultry
sizzling
smoldering
torrid

For further inspiration, see:
Physical Words

SOUNDS

Granted, some of the words on this list might look a bit silly at first glance. (All right, probably *most* of them look silly.) But never underestimate the importance of sound-related images in bringing your message to life. Alka-Seltzer scored an unforgettable triumph with its old "Plop-plop, fizz-fizz" campaign. And Rice Krispies won a permanent spot in the marketing pantheon with its catchy "snap, crackle, and pop."

Why do these odd sounds work? Anything that lifts your words off the flat surface of the page or screen will lift response. The same goes for anything that makes your message stand out in the reader's (or listener's) memory. "Sound words" are both vivid and memorable.

If you're writing a space ad or radio campaign, see if you can find a signature sound for your product. (Feel free to join two or more sound words in brave new combinations.) When you write direct-mail or Internet advertising, you can use these colorful words to add sizzle to the proverbial steak. In other words, sound words can make your message *sing*.

purr	rustle
whir	hiss
hum	sizzle
drone	fizz
buzz	pitter-patter
whine	splash
sigh	sploosh
murmur	splat
whisper	plop

splatter	cluck
splutter	chirp
sputter	cheep
grind	peep
crunch	warble
crackle	whistle
creak	tweet
rasp	twitter
roar	trill
bellow	hoot
yell	coo
shout	wail
scream	chant
screech	croon
growl	sing
howl	ring
yowl	bing
bark	ka-ching
woof	zing
yip	tinkle
yap	jingle
yelp	peal
meow	chime
mew	gong
whinny	bong
neigh	bing-bong
bleat	ding-dong
moo	knell
oink	toll
grunt	blast
squeal	toot
squeak	tootle
squawk	bugle
croak	blare
honk	rumble
quack	thunder

echo	whack
boom	thwack
kaboom	whap
bang	wham
bam	snap
crash	blap
clash	zap
smash	pop
pound	boing
drum	sproing
thud	beep
thump	yak
whump	cackle
whomp	babble
clunk	chatter
clank	yammer
plunk	snicker
strum	titter
thrum	laugh
twang	guffaw
pluck	chuckle
rap	chortle
tap	burble
knock	gurgle
rattle	gulp
clink	glug
click	gargle
clack	snort
clickety-clack	sneeze
pocketa-pocketa	wheeze
tick-tock	snore
tick-tick	zzz . . .
clip-clop	sniff
clap	sniffle
slap	snuffle
smack	whimper

whoop
whoosh
swish
swoosh
vroom
zoom

pow
poof

For further inspiration, see:
Physical Words

SUBSCRIPTION ADVERTISING

Selling the public on a magazine (or any other serial publication) can be reduced to a predictable formula. You tantalize your prospects with tasty nuggets culled from recent issues. You create a sales letter that flatters and invites your audience. You offer a free (and relevant) gift as well as a price break on the subscription *plus* an ironclad guarantee of satisfaction. You include a lift note from an authority figure to convert the hesitant. You attach (wherever possible) rave reviews from esteemed publications and individual eminentoes. You insert an inviting and easy-to-use order form. Piece of cake, right?

Not so fast. What separates inspired subscription advertising from the also-rans can be boiled down to two basic elements: excitement and imagination. No formula can help you here; it's up to you to get excited about your publication and bring that excitement to life for your audience. The phrases on this list can't provide that critical spark, but they should help your ideas start flowing. Just as important, they supply you with the nuts-and-bolts phrases that form the foundation of successful subscription advertising.

You've been selected to receive —— at our special introductory savings rate!
engagingly written
crisply written
award-winning
richly illustrated
month after month
Now you can take a closer look.
an up-close, behind-the-scenes look
Learn the stories behind the . . .
Get the real story behind the . . . .
Immerse yourself in fascinating articles.
Enjoy reading all about ——.
Enter a world of . . .
Come face-to-face with . . .
Take part in the adventure . . .

Probe the mysteries of . . .

. . . what you *don't* know about
——.

Reading —— is like taking a
monthly vacation to ——.

a stimulating grab bag of —— in
every issue

the —— that sheds light on ——

the first magazine to . . .

—— is more than a magazine
about ——.

—— is a magazine that celebrates
——.

With every issue of ——, you
discover . . .

cover-to-cover reading enjoyment

journalism that's as intelligent as
you are

If you like being surprised and
entertained, . . .

I want to share the excitement with
you.

the official publication of the
prestigious ——

the favorite magazine of ——

available now for you to sample
FREE

It all starts with your FREE issue.

more than ——,000 readers

Isn't it time you discovered ——?
Over ——,000 others just like
you already have.

All our readers have this in
common: . . .

Our subscribers are interesting and
accomplished people from all
walks of life.

The list from which we obtained
your name indicates that you're
a person who . . .

We've sent this special offer to a
select group of —— who . . .

Frankly, —— isn't for everyone.
But if my instincts are right, I
believe it's for you.

Decide for yourself if —— is right
for you.

Join our growing family of
subscribers.

When you say 'Yes!' to [name of
publication], you say 'Yes!' to
——.

I hope you'll take us up on our
invitation.

guaranteed lowest rate

——% savings off the cover
price

an incredible savings of
over ——% off the cover
price

for just $—— — ——% off the
cover price

Save ——% off the newsstand
price

as little as ——¢ a copy

New subscriber discount!

Try —— risk-free.

Enjoy the next issue free without
risk or obligation.

You're invited to try the next issue
free.

with no risk or obligation
whatsoever

No risk! No obligation!

Send no money!

Return the enclosed card to receive your free trial issue.

Just mail the token on the enclosed card.

Hurry! Mail the reply card today!

Simply return the Free Preview certificate.

Fill out the enclosed reply card and drop it in the mail today.

Fill out the enclosed reply card today or call us at ——.

Fill out the enclosed reply card today or visit us on the Web at ——.

Introductory Savings Certificate

To start enjoying ——, just check one of the options below.

Reply within —— days and receive your free ——.

Order —— today and receive a FREE ——.

Mail your order within __ days and we'll send you a FREE —— as your "welcome aboard" gift!

This handsome ——–valued at $——–is yours FREE when you order ——.

yours FREE with your paid subscription

I'll see that you receive your free issue.

We'll treat you to the next issue.

Remember, this offer is good for a limited time only.

For faster service, order online at ——.

Please allow —— weeks for delivery of your first issue.

If you wish to continue receiving —— after your free trial, we'll be happy to send you another —— issues for just $——.

It costs nothing to find out whether —— is for you.

When you subscribe to ——, your satisfaction is 100% guaranteed.

If you're not absolutely delighted with ——, just let us know and we'll refund 100% of your payment.

Just notify us at any time and we'll refund your entire subscription price.

If you decide that —— is not for you, just write "cancel" on your invoice and owe nothing.

Since you risk absolutely nothing, why not say "Yes!" to ——?

Since there's no risk, why not sign up for *two* years and save an additional $——?

Renew your subscription now and we'll send you . . .

Give a full year of —— to someone you care about.

For further inspiration, see:
Verbs (especially "Discover" and "Persuade/Decide")

TECHNOLOGY ADVERTISING

Tech advertising is like tightrope-walking: a fine line between dangerous extremes. On the one hand, you don't want to sound mundane; you need to dazzle your readers with the cutting-edge possibilities of your product or organization. On the other hand, you don't want to leave your audience in the dust, dumbfounded and uncomprehending. The true path is a narrow one—the mean between the extremes.

It helps to know your audience, as it always does in any form of advertising. If you're speaking directly to information technology professionals, for example, you can cut loose and fling all manner of buzzwords at their receptive eyes. If you're addressing nontechnical managers or general consumers, it's best not to get carried away with technospeak. In either case, remember that the *benefits* of your glittery features, not the features themselves, are going to carry the day for you.

This section begins with a list of frequently used tech terms to keep in mind as you write. The longer phrases that follow should come in handy as you craft your copy.

Caution: I probably don't have to remind you that the vocabulary of technology mutates as rapidly as teenage slang. Today's state-of-the-art buzzword is tomorrow's antique. (That goes for "state-of-the-art," too.) Keep this list updated by adding new terms as you hear them and crossing off the more dated ones.

ultimate	customized
cutting-edge	customizable
leading-edge	expandable
optimized	enhanced
personalized	advanced

equipped	bundle
dedicated	upgrade
connected	fine-tune
automatic	troubleshoot
sleek	delivers
powerful	transforms
global	maximizes
digital	minimizes
optical	high-speed
streaming	high-capacity
real-time	high-definition
embedded	high-resolution
encrypted	high-performance
broadband	kilo——
bandwidth	mega——
network	giga——
networking	tera——
surfing	nano——
gaming	downloadable
multimedia	quickly download
navigation	download with ease
cyberspace	——-enabled
interconnectivity	——-ready
functionality	——-friendly
performance	——-compatible
flexibility	—— on demand
imaging	advanced ——
interface	enhanced ——
settings	smart ——
mode	instant information
module	access to critical
system	information
database	whenever and wherever
platform	retrieve data
accessories	speed and efficiency
applications	speed and power
peripherals	faster than ever

blazing fast
You're always connected.
links your existing infrastructure
    to . . .
works seamlessly with virtually
    any system
expertly configured
easy to install
tool-free installation
up and running within minutes
plug-and-play
puts —— within reach at all times
navigate with ease
store your preferences
Manage all your —— from a single
    site.
a complete —— solution
built-in ——
puts —— in the palm of your hand
puts —— right on your desktop
combines lightweight versatility
    with heavyweight performance
totally mobile

explore your options
delivers amazing performance
breathtaking realism
incredible visuals
top-of-the-line
sets the standard
industry-standard technology
a huge step forward in ——
    technology
on top of the rapidly moving
    technology curve
the latest ——
the revolutionary way to . . .
Protect your computer data!
powerful software
backed by the power of ——
powered by ——
24-hour support
We walk you through every step.

For further inspiration, see:
**Online Marketing Services; Web
Copy**

TEXTURES

How do you describe the feel of a product that your readers can't touch? By choosing *words* they can touch.

Maybe your reader can see the product in your catalog photos. Your copy description helps complete the picture. But you can bring that picture to life by helping your reader touch the item through your words. How does the product feel when you hold it? What does its surface remind you of? By describing the texture of a product, you help the reader experience what it would be like to own it. And that's a powerful selling advantage.

The first part of this list is a fairly thorough catalog of textures, from furry to crunchy to misty. Notice that similar textures are grouped together for easy searching. The second part of the list helps you compare the texture of your product to something the reader will instantly recognize. This section is nowhere close to exhaustive, since the world is full of wondrous and intriguing textures that remind you of *other* textures. But it should help you get started.

furry	nubby
hairy	stubbly
shaggy	frizzy
feathery	nappy
downy	kinky
fuzzy	wavy
woolly	curly
fleecy	coarse
tweedy	rugged

tough	smooth
rough	matte finish
rough-hewn	mellow finish
jagged	semigloss
craggy	polished
weathered	varnished
dry	glazed
parched	buffed
sunbaked	glossy
leathery	glassy
leatherlike	sleek
richly grained	slick
richly embossed	shiny
deeply embossed	sparkling
richly textured	glittering
crinkly	gleaming
crinkled	lustrous
crunchy	burnished
crackly	metallic
crackled	flaky
crisp	flecked
crispy	mottled
brittle	pebbled
chipped	pebbly
shredded	gritty
chopped	sandy
minced	grainy
grated	granulated
pureed	fine-grained
scalloped	powdered
undulating	powdery
serrated	dusty
razor-sharp	soft
sharp-edged	tender
angled	fluffy
hard	lacy
firm	cushiony

padded

plush

supple

elastic

pliable

silky

silken

velvety

foamy

spongy

pulpy

squishy

creamy

buttery

greasy

fatty

oily

oiled

beaded

liquid

flowing

rippling

wet

damp

moist

milky

syrupy

sticky

chewy

fudgy

gooey

gummy

waxy

tacky

foggy

steamy

steaming

cloudy

vaporous

misty

The texture of . . .

slush

snow cones

Italian ice

creamy gelato

sorbet

snow

ice

glass

marble

granite

gravel

sandstone

sandpaper

parchment

tissue paper

manila paper

handmade paper

cardboard

canvas

burlap

cotton

fine linen

silk

satin

velvet

felt

a worsted suit

fine-grained calfskin

full-grained cowhide

expensive leather upholstery

polished mahogany

pine bark

a shiny apple
an orange rind
peach fuzz
woodland moss
goose down
peacock feathers
lambswool
cashmere
mohair
an Irish fisherman's sweater
deep-pile carpeting
the most costly mink
a baby's behind
Jell-O
pudding
custard
yogurt
crème brûlée
molasses
caramel
butter

creamy peanut butter
milk chocolate
cookie dough
wet cement
mud
modeling clay
rich soil
multigrain bread
potato skins
mashed potatoes
oatmeal
grits
shredded wheat
corn flakes
crispy bacon
caviar
filet mignon

For further inspiration, see:
Flavors; Fragrances; Physical Words

UPSCALE WORDS

Yes, these dressy words and phrases should elicit a positive response from upmarket prospects when you're selling expensive and finely crafted products. But this list will also serve you when you need to appeal to the general reader's class aspirations. Who among us hasn't, at one time or another, dreamed of leading an aristocratic lifestyle with all the trappings? Even in our dress-down, post-WASP society, the pursuit of class is still a powerful motivator.

Notice that I haven't included the word *classy* on the list. For one, it's too vague. More important, it's not an especially classy word. (Think of a 1930s gangster looking around the room and muttering, "Geez, what a classy joint!")

polished	fine
refined	precious
urbane	costly
regal	priceless
aristocratic	antique
patrician	detailing
distinguished	amenities
opulent	accoutrements
stately	richly appointed
luxurious	meticulously handcrafted
sumptuous	hand-tooled
magnificent	handwrought
masterpiece	Old World craftsmanship
rare	museum quality
noble	heirloom quality

premium quality	wry
superior	witty
superlative	acerbic
exquisite	jaded
harmonious	bestow
elegant	bequeath
timeless	inherit
classic	savor
venerable	value
a legacy of . . .	treasure
finesse	esteem
panache	honor
élan	admire
verve	acquire
cachet	discriminating
glamour	exacting
distinction	demanding
elite	understated grace and elegance
cosmopolitan	perfectly proportioned
urbane	for the discriminating few
worldly	held in high regard
sporty	found only at the finest ——
dapper	our exacting standards
debonair	. . . for generations
dressy	flagrantly expensive
uptown	an obvious extravagance
chic	an affordable extravagance
prestigious	unabashed luxury
respected	a ____ of obvious distinction
esteemed	Your ____ says a lot about you.
renowned	what sets you apart
legendary	a world of privilege
gifted	This offer is available to only a
intelligent	select few.
Ivy League	
literate	*For further inspiration, see:*
droll	**Personal Qualities**

VERBS

If nouns are the backbone of your writing, verbs provide the muscle. You can't get from here to there without them. We tend to fall back on a handful of mundane verbs like *is* and *get*—and that's fine up to a point. (*Get* is actually a highly effective verb in advertising.) But if you really want your copy to crackle, sparkle, and sing, use strong verbs like *crackle*, *sparkle*, and *sing*.

How do you develop a sense for sniffing out strong verbs? Here's my rule of thumb: favor earthy Anglo-Saxon verbs over those of Latin origin. Think of *eat* versus *ingest*, or *drink* versus *imbibe*. True, many Latin-based verbs are indispensable (and I've honored them in this list), so don't take my advice to extremes. But remember that most of our borrowed Latinisms tend to sound more cerebral and pack less of an emotional punch than our native English words.

A comprehensive listing of verbs could fill an entire book. I've whittled down the choices for you: just the most useful verbs and verb phrases, clustered into twenty alphabetically arranged categories for easy selection. Simply scan the categories for the concept you want, then pick your verb from that list. Happy hunting!

Assist

offer
supply
provide
bring you
give you
equip you with
outfit you with
furnish you with
go to bat for
help
aid
boost
lend a hand
guide
advise
coach
consult

pitch in	live
contribute	thrive
support	flourish
subsidize	grow
serve	mature
obey	mellow
listen	think
report to	reflect
participate	feel
cooperate	lurk
collaborate	loaf
team up with	hang out
join forces with	relax
partner with	rest
combine	unwind
fuse	continue
synergize	endure
harmonize	accept
mesh	embrace
meld	encompass
unite	include
bring together	contain
share	comprise
nurture	consist of
nurse	fit
nourish	occupy
feed	embody
foster	represent
devote	stand for
dedicate	symbolize
facilitate	illustrate
expedite	

Be

	Consume
	get
seem	gain
appear	earn
exist	win

obtain
order
shop
buy
spend
purchase
splurge
acquire
collect
pick up
rack up
gather
amass
supplement
round out
fill out
build
add
download
upgrade
borrow
use
try
enjoy
savor
relish
taste
nibble
graze
eat
feast
gobble
put away
dine
gulp
drink
sip

imbibe
devour
take
wear
outfit
stock up
arm yourself with
take advantage of
treat yourself to

Create

imagine
conceive
picture
dream
dream up
brainstorm
plan
think
contemplate
prepare
propose
design
organize
outline
draft
sketch
compose
model
plot
program
formulate
fashion
invent
devise
develop
emerge

beget
hatch
spawn
give birth to
germinate
make
forge
concoct
shape
mold
generate
build
manufacture
construct
assemble
put together
produce
engineer
mint
introduce
inaugurate
announce
proclaim
herald
release
unleash
roll out
crank out
copy
reproduce
duplicate
clone

Dazzle/Excite

sparkle
glitter
shimmer

glow
radiate
smolder
titillate
scintillate
ignite
stir
brighten
beguile
appeal
entice
enthrall
enchant
delight
entertain
intrigue
attract
seduce
tempt
tantalize
caress
embrace
tingle
mesmerize
bewitch
captivate
thrill
amaze
astound
astonish
wallop
electrify
sizzle
burst
erupt
shatter
explode

provoke
challenge
shock
stun
shiver
shudder
surprise
startle
chill
wonder

Defy

challenge
brave
combat
contend
dispute
oppose
confront
intercept
shoot down
debunk
frustrate
baffle
foil
thwart
stymie
mystify
dare
shock
mock
taunt
scorn
argue
bicker
squabble
quibble

protest
block
provoke
push
flout
fight
battle
resist
defend
fend off
grapple with
wrangle
struggle
deny
ignore
snub
dismiss
decline
turn a deaf ear to
elude
evade
dodge
escape
avoid
lurk
intrude
threaten

Discover

seek
search
hunt
rummage
inspect
investigate
venture
quest

delve

dig

sniff out

snoop

spy

pry

probe

plumb

penetrate

explore

journey

navigate

voyage

chart your course

encounter

uncover

unlock

unearth

decode

decipher

reveal

behold

meet

find

learn

absorb

transcend

master

solve

solve the riddle of . . .

cross over into . . .

take the leap

tap into . . .

see

observe

witness

visualize

awaken

inspire

evoke

experience

unleash

soar

rediscover

recall

relive

Eliminate/Defeat

save

simplify

clarify

streamline

trim

reduce

minimize

diminish

downsize

downgrade

deplete

dilute

drain

sap

prune

whittle down

shorten

shave

slash

split

divide

subtract

detach

dismantle

untangle

disperse

reverse
relieve
ease
relax
lighten
soothe
banish
repel
knock
block
tackle
fight
smash
crush
squash
quash
slam
whip
beat
drub
rout
trounce
wallop
pulverize
overpower
overwhelm
subdue
thwart
foil
hammer
blow away
whisk away
cut
cut through
cut down on
break
stop

kill
stamp out
shut out
wipe out
wipe away
remove
erase
omit
neglect
void
scrap
ditch
jettison
shed
drop
toss
unload
obliterate
get rid of
take no prisoners

Enhance

embellish
decorate
adorn
enrich
cultivate
foster
grow
advance
expand
stretch
extend
boost
raise
lift
heighten

amplify
refine
fine-tune
improve
upgrade
step up to
move up to
excel
exceed
surpass
outshine
outdo
double
triple
transform
promote
produce
energize
strengthen
fortify
toughen
reinforce
revitalize
refresh
rejuvenate
revive
renew
refurbish
renovate
revamp
overhaul
rebuild
rekindle
restore
repair
fix
mend

touch up
correct

Enjoy

appreciate
admire
value
treasure
relish
savor
indulge
bask
luxuriate
rejoice
flip
romp
play
sing
dance
shout
celebrate
revel
frolic
have fun
treat yourself
free yourself
whoop it up
party
make noise
make merry
get down
get away
escape
break out

Fail

disappoint

decline
deflate
droop
drop
sag
sink
goof
botch
bungle
muff
miss
retreat
slip
slip up
stumble
tumble
fumble
crumble
surrender
give in
lose
fall
fold
flop
flail
founder
flounder
blunder
swoon
shrink
fizzle
abort
wither
fade
languish
perish
expire

ruin
bankrupt
embarrass
humiliate
mortify
belittle
disgrace
be ridiculed
be discredited
be insulted
be snubbed
be duped
be fooled
be trapped
be tricked
be hoodwinked
be taken for a ride
fall short
sound a retreat
hit bottom
shut down
break down
run aground
crash and burn
go up in smoke
go belly up

Function

use
make use of
act
work
tackle
take on
deliver
provide
include

gather

cull

store

contain

have

hold

fit

put

suit

apply

compensate

adapt

convert

switch

swap

change

turn —— into ——

simulate

reproduce

multiply

add

subtract

divide

separate

diminish

split

transfer

furnish

give

take

grab

seize

haul

push

pull

stretch

sharpen

dull

freeze

melt

pass

distribute

solve

identify

pinpoint

focus

combine

blend

meld

mesh

mix

link

join

start

begin

curtail

limit

maintain

control

demonstrate

illustrate

Go/Move

stir

budge

start

set out

drift

flow

swim

paddle

inch

crawl

wiggle

wriggle
squirm
slither
slide
waddle
wobble
ramble
plod
prowl
step
walk
stroll
stride
prance
march
hike
swagger
bustle
rush
scramble
zip
gallop
sprint
churn
twist
turn
rotate
revolve
spin
twirl
shake
rattle
roll
glide
drive
dart
dash

speed
zoom
rocket
blast
fly
flutter
soar
plunge
tumble
slam
smash
crash
bounce
jiggle
twitch
quiver
quake
rumble
vibrate
discharge
hit
pierce
enter
open
close
shut
stop
halt
go to it
go for it
make your move
get a move on

Include

contain
provide
provides you with . . .

feature

offer

offers you . . .

outfit

outfits you with . . .

equip

equips you with . . .

pack

packs all this into . . .

fill

filled with . . .

give

gives you all this . . .

serve up

comprise

embrace

encompass

put together

bring together

combine

assemble

assembles —— into one

    convenient ——

receive

get

deliver

insert

infuse

Manage

administer

arrange

orchestrate

spearhead

control

monitor

check

review

examine

observe

look in on

operate

oversee

run

supervise

guide

steer

head

lead

preside

influence

initiate

inaugurate

establish

create

develop

decide

apply

negotiate

implement

carry out

execute

command

enforce

achieve

perform

interface

interact

evaluate

weigh

approve

allocate

authorize

assign

appoint
enable
mentor
delegate
support
streamline

Persuade/Decide

propose
consider
compare
influence
motivate
move
impress
urge
insist
speak out
speak up
recommend
endorse
advocate
vouch
prove
affirm
attest
advise
assure
trust
invite
appeal
ask
beg
plead
implore
judge
weigh

discern
discriminate
determine
act
respond
agree
give in
concede
reciprocate
accept
acknowledge
approve
commit
choose
pick
select
opt for
cull
order
subscribe
visit
drop by
drop in
come on out
support
conclude
hesitate
decline
dismiss
reject

Say

chat
chatter
gab
schmooze
shoot the breeze

whisper	plead
speak	beg
speak up	inquire
speak out	quiz
announce	grill
note	question
discuss	lament
discourse	disapprove
comment	quibble
promise	whine
pledge	grumble
explain	grouse
spell out	scold
express	scoff
observe	sneer
suggest	snicker
hint	jeer
imply	needle
confide	attack
remark	lash out
voice	hurl barbs
articulate	diss
assert	denounce
confirm	blast
order	slam
approve	satirize
cheer	offend
greet	swear
welcome	insult
flatter	slander
tout	libel
praise	smear
acclaim	revile
applaud	lambaste
commend	ridicule
okay	taunt
ask	write off

cut down to size
ramble
prattle
babble
preach
squawk
screech
blab
yack
hoot
holler
yell
shout
rant
rave

Secure/Guarantee

assure
ensure
insure
prevent
protect
defend
fend off
ward off
guard
safeguard
guard against
shield
reinforce
confirm
attest
testify
affirm
entrust
trust
authorize

warrant
certify
validate
entitle
retain
remind
remember
alert
monitor
shelter
insulate
conceal
stash
hide
disguise
camouflage
encode
embed
encrypt
cover

Succeed

perform
master
gain
surge
follow through
make it
pay off
earn
reap
profit
capitalize
sell
score
accomplish
fulfill

benefit	value
surpass	prize
outshine	prefer
outscore	desire
outclass	aspire
outrank	yearn
outstrip	flirt
outperform	tease
outlast	anticipate
outdistance	expect
track	need
pursue	crave
chase	ache
aim	obsess
shoot for . . .	demand
capture	require
nab	must have
snatch	insist on
catch	long for
solve	hunger for
resolve	burn with
achieve	lust after
win	can't live without
beat	take
overcome	grab
triumph	seize
conquer	possess
summit	enjoy
come out on top	relish
	savor
Want/Love	cherish
wish	adore
dream	idolize
hope	
like	*For further inspiration, see:*
be fond of	**Physical Words; Sounds**

WEB COPY

If you think about it, your website is an extended advertisement and branding statement for your organization. It can be a catalog, a direct-response package, and a corporate image ad all rolled into one. Above all, it's an *interactive* ad. Never before has any medium offered such amazing possibilities for helping your customers connect with you. Aside from ordering your products, they can learn about your history, get acquainted with your staff, offer valuable feedback, and even check for employment opportunities.

This list won't provide you with actual site content. (After all, websites are as diverse as the companies behind them.) Instead, it includes the phrases you need on your home page to invite interaction from visitors. Most successful sites use a fairly standard assortment of clickable hyperlinked phrases for this purpose.

I've visited a few dozen of the most successful sites and captured these phrases for your use. You'll see some alternate wordings of the same feature; just choose the one that sounds best to you. Even if your site is already up and running (and running successfully), you can scan this list for features that might be worth adding.

Welcome to ——!
Hello, [name of customer]!
[name of customer], check out
   what's new for you.
[name of customer], click here
   for your sneak preview.
Home
About Us

Company Info
Company Profile
Our Mission
Online Catalog
Our Store
Clearance Center
Sale Annex
Today's Specials

Free Downloads
Log-in
Sign In
Register Here
Register Now
My Account
Your Account
My [name of site]
Edit Preferences
Shopping Cart
View Cart
Want List
Go to Checkout
Keep Shopping
Gift Certificates
Gift Subscriptions
Tip of the Day
Today's News
In the News
Site Map
Site Index
Tools
Categories
Featured Items
Marketplace
Products
Services
Corporate Sales
Investor Relations
Customer Service
Employment Opportunities
Career Opportunities
Careers
Jobs
Our Staff
Our Crew
Community

Media
Partners
Announcements
Terms and Conditions
User Agreement
Returns Policy
Privacy Policy
Legal Notices
Advertise
Advertise in ——
Frequently Asked Questions
    (FAQ)
Store Location(s)
Store Locator
Directions
Contact Us
Contacts
E-Mail a Friend
Feedback
Quick Links
Help
Search for:
Join
Order
Click Here
Find It
Go
Only from ——!
Special for our online customers
    only!
Take ——% off your entire order!
Be sure to check out our ——.
New to ——?
Open an account.
Check product availability.
Check your order status.
Join our affiliate program.

Request our catalog.
Price match guarantee
Customer reviews
Share your thoughts with our
   community.
Create a personal ———.
E-mail this page to a friend.
Bookmark this page.
Add this page to your favorites.
Make us your home page.
Click to enlarge.

See more ———.
Enter your E-mail address for free
   bulletins.
Subscribe to our E-mail newsletter.
Now in stock!
More great deals . . .

For further inspiration, see:
Online Marketing Services;
Technology Advertising;
Appendix D: Online Copy

YOUTH MARKET

Trying to reach a young audience? You want your words to crackle with energy and a dash of irreverence. Today's youth market is impatient with low-energy, abstract verbiage and receptive to high-impact, sensory images. Think of skateboards, video games, and caffeine as you create your message.

The words on this list have been mined from sports, pop music, Internet lingo, and other sources of youthspeak. But the lexicon of youth is constantly reinventing itself beyond our radar. Be careful not to use once-trendy expressions that kids could dismiss with a sniffy "That's *so* six months ago!"

I've tried to compile words that stand a reasonable chance of survival—at least for the next six months. (Actually, many of them are older terms that have established a niche in our language.) You might want to customize this list by adding cool new phrases as you hear them and crossing off the ones that seem hopelessly dated.

Caution: Don't pander to the young by overloading your copy with words from this list. Instead, use them sparingly to give your message a more contemporary and youth-friendly feel.

break out	slam
blow the lid off	slam-dunk
blow away	swoosh
blowout	slap
blitz	speed
explode	rev up
blast	crank up
smash	turbocharge

morph
rock
Rock your ——.
—— rocks!
—— rules!
check it out
mouth off
kick butt
play to win
swipe
grab
catch the ——
in the zone
—— zone
—— machine
off the charts
the next level
awesome
amazing
outrageous
edgy
cool
hot
hottest
smoking
blazing
sizzling
unreal
ultimate
wired
juiced
in-your-face
hard-hitting
jaw-dropping
bone-crushing

pulse-pounding
ground-pounding
mega——
cyber——
monster ——
mutant ——
stealth ——
killer ——
extreme ——
outlaw ——
guerrilla ——
flat-out ——
—— gone bad
shock wave
sound wave
electric
buzz
neon
heat
juice
juju
mojo
baddest
nasty
takes no prisoners
bulletproof
with attitude
fave
yeah
dude
whatever

For further inspiration, see:
**Emotional Words; Physical
Words; Sexy Words; Verbs**

APPENDIX A

Your Personal Copy Checklist

Nothing disrupts a copywriter's already-fitful sleep like the suspicion that a crucial mailing has gone out the door with something amiss. Before you turn your copy over to the client or printer, check it against the following list to make sure you haven't forgotten anything essential.

- ☐ All facts are accurate.

- ☐ Copy has been edited for errors in grammar, spelling, and punctuation.

- ☐ All typos have been corrected.

- ☐ You've styled variable terms (e.g., e-mail, E-mail, Email) consistently throughout.

- ☐ You've maintained a consistent writing style throughout.

- ☐ Copy is geared to the target audience.

- ☐ Provocative teaser copy makes it virtually impossible to toss or delete your ad.

- ☐ Headlines emphasize product benefits forcefully and succinctly.

- ☐ Benefits and selling points are stated clearly, prominently, and persuasively throughout the copy.

- ☐ Any page breaks occur in midsentence so reader is led to next page.

- ☐ Copy holds the reader's interest from start to finish.

☐ All verbiage that doesn't contribute to the effectiveness of the copy has been weeded out.

☐ You've broken up long copy with intriguing subheads.

☐ You've presented all product options: colors, sizes, styles, accessories.

☐ You've supplied current prices and product numbers.

☐ You've included endorsements from customers and/or celebrities where available.

☐ The reader has just enough information to make a decision—not less, not more.

☐ Copy includes a forceful call to action.

☐ You've told the reader how to order.

☐ Your company name, address, contact information, and guarantee are clearly visible.

☐ You would be proud to sign your name to this copy.

☐ The customer would look forward to receiving similar advertising in the future.

APPENDIX B

Twenty-Five Common Copywriting Pitfalls (and How to Avoid Them)

Writing copy is like crossing a minefield: so many opportunities for self-destruction! The experienced copywriter knows where most of the mines are hidden and can usually step around them with grace and skill. But all of us stumble from time to time.

Think of this section as your personal map of the "minefield"—so you can pinpoint the most treacherous spots, sidestep them, and reach your destination in one piece. I begin with common advertising copy blunders, then move on to general writing pitfalls.

1. **Unsuitable tone.** Don't assault a mass market audience with words like *egregious*, and don't resort to razzle-dazzle hucksterism with upscale readers. Try to understand the needs and tastes of the people you're addressing, and write as if you're one of them—only a little more persuasive.

2. **Unbelievable claims.** Credibility is like a necklace: break the strand at any point and all the beads go scattering. When you introduce even one dubious claim into your sales pitch, the thread of credibility snaps and your readers may reject your entire argument. Always be prepared to support your claims with irrefutable evidence.

3. **Wrong information.** Probably the most serious blunder, but also one of the easiest to fix. Simply check your facts—including product features, colors, styles, sizes, product numbers, and prices—before you submit your copy.

4. **Conflicting information.** You can't tell your audience to "send no money" in one paragraph, then promise a full refund in your guarantee. (After all, you can't refund money they haven't sent.) Make sure your copy doesn't give off mixed messages.

5. **Buried information.** Don't lead your audience on a long treasure hunt for benefits and key facts. Introduce these early and keep developing them, so you create the motivation your readers need to follow you all the way to the payoff.

6. **Missing information.**

7. **Self-indulgent copy.** One of the cardinal sins of copywriting—and one of the most tempting. Most of us who write copy enjoy playing with words, and that's commendable. But always remember that your writing must serve the sales pitch, and not vice versa. Use your talents to write clean, clear prose that motivates the reader. If you still crave self-expression, you can indulge your literary muse by lamplight when your work is done.

8. **Company-indulgent copy.** Here the company is the hero, strutting and posturing like a peacock. Instead of trying to impress your readers, try to *convince* them. It's not "See how great we are," but "See what we can do for you."

9. **Excessive throat clearing.** A common malady, especially among letter writers. Given the deluge of mail the average consumer receives today, your message should take no more than five to ten seconds of the reader's time to make its point—or it will surely get tossed. (Letter writers: A powerful headline or overline message above the salutation takes some of the pressure off the first paragraph and lets you ease into your sales pitch with a beguiling anecdote.)

10. **Inappropriate humor.** While TV and radio advertising have always used humor to advantage, direct-response advertising is, for better or worse, a fundamentally humorless medium. (There's little time for horseplay when you have to close a sale.) You definitely want to avoid puns, jokes, and any other rib-ticklers of the "Get it? Get it?" variety. On the other hand, subtle humor can be an effective way to disarm your readers and create rapport. But gauge your audience first, and tread with caution.

11. **No call to action.** Direct-response advertising without a call to action is like a mystery novel without a denouement, a 3–3 baseball game without a tie-breaking hit, love without marriage. The call to action is what converts browsing readers into buyers. Unless you remind them to call/click/drop that card in the mail, they'll just move on to somebody else's pasture.

12. **Unfocused language.** Like a blurred photograph, unfocused copy lacks detail and clarity. A statement like "We offer stylish clothes" transmits a lazy, hazy image to the reader. Stylish in what sense? Glamorous? Funky and outrageous? Classic preppie? Don't just hint at an image and make your readers do the work. (They won't.) Go the extra step to enhance the picture and bring it into sharp focus for your audience.

13. **Word repetitions within close range.** Try to avoid sentences like "These colorful memos come in a multicolored assortment of six assorted colors." Our language has more than enough synonyms to go around. (**Note:** When you change one of the words, check the sentences in the immediate vicinity to make sure you haven't already used it there.) Deliberate repetitions for emphasis ("The best materials. The best prices. The best service.") are perfectly acceptable.

14. **Comma between subject and verb.** You know the problem: "This solar-powered calculator, is the greatest invention since the abacus." It sounds petty, but little mistakes like this can make your copy look amateurish. Never use a comma to separate the subject and verb unless you're marking off a subordinate clause that falls between them. (A fairly good rule of thumb is to insert a comma only where you'd pause when you read the sentence aloud.)

15. **Subject/verb nonagreement.** This one's obvious, you might think. A man shaves; men shave. What could be simpler? But watch out for tricky sentences like the following: "Every one of these unforgettable books celebrates [not *celebrate*] the written word." The verb doesn't automatically agree with the closest noun; it has to agree with the subject of the sentence. If the subject is singular (in this case, *one*), so is the verb. It's "Every one . . . celebrates."

16. **Dangling participles.** This all-too-common blunder can produce some grotesquely comical effects, such as "Driving down the road, your heart

leaps with excitement." (Let's hope your heart has a driver's license!) Remember that the participle (in this case, *driving*) must refer to the subject of the sentence (*heart*). Since hearts don't drive, you might change the sentence to read "As you drive down the road, your heart leaps with excitement." Or you could keep the participle and change the subject of the sentence to *you*: "Driving down the road, you feel a rush of excitement."

17. **Pile-on prepositional phrases.** And now for a word of advice from the author to writers of copy in the interest of clarity in advertising: please avoid sentences like this one. Restructure your thoughts and find an alternate route.

18. **Interminably long sentences.** Don't write 'em.

19. **Ambiguous modifiers.** Beware of adjectives that can modify two words at once, as in this hypothetical auto supply store's message to its preferred customers: "Private Parts Sale." Obviously, it's the sale that's private and not the parts, but the sentence fails to clarify the matter.

20. **Misuse of "quotation marks."** We've all seen those hand-painted signs for "Farm-Fresh" Eggs (or worse yet, Farm-Fresh "Eggs"). Never use quotation marks for emphasis. (You can use underlines or all caps or italics, but not quotes.) In this context, quotation marks give the impression that the enclosed words aren't to be taken literally. (If you refer to eggs as "eggs," what are they *really*?)

21. **Confusion of *it's* and *its*.** Here's the distinction: *It's* (with an apostrophe) is a contraction of *it is*. (It's plain to see. It's never too late. It's in the bag.) When you want it to be possessive, always use *its*—no apostrophe. (Note its sleek profile. Feel its rich leather interior.) I know it seems odd to form a possessive without an apostrophe, but that's the way it is with *its*.

22. **Confusion of *you're* and *your*.** Same deal here. *You're* (with apostrophe) is a contraction of *you are* (You're the one for this job). By contrast, *your* is always possessive (Your friend wants your job).

23. **Passive voice.** The voice of weariness and indifference. Sometimes *it can't be avoided*, but with a little extra thought, *you can avoid it*. Use active verbs and let them carry the sentence.

24. **Faulty punctuation of internal phrases and clauses.** Some folks have no respect for punctuation; they'll throw in a comma or leave it out as it suits them. But keep in mind that punctuation is the reader's key to sentence structure and meaning. When you interrupt a sentence with a subordinate clause or phrase, you mark it off with punctuation—either a pair of commas or a pair of dashes—so the reader knows where the main part of the sentence stops and where it resumes. Just like that.

25. **Etc.** Don't force your audience to read your mind, finish your sentences for you, etc. There are more creative ways to present a partial list of features. If you're promoting a musical anthology of great singers, for example, you can write, "The collection spans a full century of recorded sound, from Caruso to Eminem." Or wrap up a partial list with "and these are just a few." Use *etc.* only in the tightest nuts-and-bolts catalog copy. Even then, it creates the impression of sketchiness, laziness, amateurism, etc.

APPENDIX C

How to Fine-Tune Your Style

et's face it: advertising is not literature of the highest order. It's not *Moby Dick* or *The Iliad*. Two centuries from now, our work might be dusted off by an occasional scholar of pop culture, but it's too much to expect that anyone will ever read it for pleasure.

But for those of us who write advertising copy, the challenge is more immediate: to use words in a manner that persuades a contemporary audience to part with a portion of its discretionary income. In fact, you might say that advertising confirms the power of words to move people's minds.

Those words—those raw materials of language—await the deft hand that, like old Rumpelstiltskin, can spin them into gold. This book supplies you with the raw materials. How you spin them, though, is just as essential to the success of your work. And that's what we mean by style.

Style demands both discipline and imagination, left-brain logic and right-brain artistry. A successful writing style is like a garden that shifts colors and patterns with the seasons, but requires a steady hand to guide and nurture it. You can't create style overnight. Most of us don't master it even in a lifetime. But with a little talent, still more work, and a few guidelines like the ones that follow, you can develop a writing style that serves your all-important message and beguiles your audience.

- **Learn the elements of sentence structure.** I will always be indebted to my sixth-grade teacher, Mrs. Umholtz, for instructing us in the art of diagramming sentences. To dissect what seemed like a random string of words and discover the underlying structure—subject, predicate, direct and indirect objects, conjunctions, subordinate clauses, prepositional phrases—was a wondrous and eye-opening experience. I heartily recommend it. Buy yourself a good guide to English grammar and usage so you can understand the inner workings of our language.

- **Put the emphasis on clarity.** In advertising, this is possibly even more important than word magic. Your readers can't act on your offer until they understand it. And they won't be able to understand it unless you explain it to them clearly. Seasoned copywriters will always swallow their pride and opt for clarity over creative expression.

- **Use colorful words to energize your copy.** Make a habit of combing your copy and substituting colorful words for limp or fuzzy ones. (This book should be able to help you in that department.) Short, lean, gritty native English words (like *short*, *lean*, and *gritty*) still pack a wallop. Words derived from Latin and Greek (such as *efficient*, *productive*, and *harmonious*) tend to sound more abstract and cerebral. Favor the native English vocabulary when you want to create a dramatic impression. Turn to our Greco-Latin heritage when you strive for erudition and precision.

- **Be aware of rhythm.** Vary your sentence structure to create a lively, flowing movement that carries the reader effortlessly downstream. Use dashes here and there to introduce exciting shifts and turns. For dramatic impact, follow a long sentence with a short, taut one. Or inject an occasional sentence fragment. For emphasis. Copy rhythm is an intuitive matter, so it's not easy to learn (or teach). Like jazz, it's something you have to feel.

- **Watch for "stoppers."** Avoid words or phrases that make the reader ponder, hesitate, backtrack, or otherwise retreat from the message. A stopper temporarily breaks the writer's hold on the reader, and that can be fatal—especially in advertising. So, in the interest of clarity and readability, be on the lookout for stoppers and banish them from your copy.

- **Favor the specific over the general.** Most stand-up comics would agree that *New Jersey* is funnier and more evocative than *a Middle Atlantic state*. The more specific you can make your language, the more impact it will have. I can't overemphasize the importance of creating sharp, well-defined images in the reader's mind.

- **Govern the flow of your copy.** Tight copy works best in tight places (like catalogs), but it can make letters a chore to read. On the other hand, free-flowing copy can work wonders in letters, but you'll want to cut the verbiage where space is at a premium. Whether tight or flowing, all copy should be economical: don't use more words than you need to create your effect.

- **Adapt your style to the product and audience.** Use a traditional upscale voice to sell fine jewelry. Adopt a warm, earnest, and slightly outraged tone when you promote a charity. If you're advertising video games, turbocharge your copy to reach the mind of a teenage male. For women's beauty products, slip into something more sensuous. Language is wonderfully supple, and you can bend it to appeal to the desires of your audience.

- **Maintain consistency of voice within a single piece.** In other words, don't launch a sales letter with a folksy anecdote and then switch to a tone of steely, gray-suited determination. Your audience is more aware of your image than you think. Some experts will tell you that *all* the copy you write for a given company should have the same tone. But you don't have to be that rigid. A newsletter shouldn't sound like a sales letter, and a sales letter shouldn't read like a brochure. Still, keep this in mind: when you do adjust your voice, try to sound like the same person in a different mood.

- **Read your mail.** Here's an opportunity for a little free education. Go through your unsolicited correspondence (we don't dare call it junk mail) and pick out the offers that catch your attention. First read them as a consumer and see if you're tempted to buy. Then review the same pieces critically and try to determine what evoked—or failed to evoke—a positive response. It's worth noting that the most effective pieces aren't always the most eloquently written.

- **Read widely.** Don't limit your critical reading to ads and professional literature. Dip into the collected works of noted essayists and journalists. Browse through highbrow and mass market magazines—and note the differences in style. Read an occasional novel or short story with a critical eye. Check out a variety of websites for writing styles that seem to hit the mark. And don't confine your explorations to writers of the moment. The great authors of the past won't necessarily serve as models for crisp, contemporary advertising copy, but they'll fill you with awe and enthusiasm for the rich possibilities of language.

- **Know when to break the rules—and when not to.** Sometimes you're entitled to take a break from the discipline of nuts-and-bolts, benefits-oriented advertising. When the image of a product is more important than what the product can do (think of fragrances or teen fashions), the main benefit is the aura of class or coolness or sexiness your product will confer on the consumer. Then you can romance your image until it wafts from the page (or screen) like some rare and costly perfume. But if your customers look to you for solutions to specific problems, your copy should offer those solutions—not mere images.

APPENDIX D

Online Copy: A Brief but Marginally Useful Primer

Banner Ads. *Miniature electronic billboards that blink, flash, display cutting-edge animation, and entice the Web surfer to click (with a convenient link to your site, of course).*

The infamous Internet bubble-burst deflated the banner ad market like a leaky tire. Don't abandon hope, though; banner ads aren't dead just yet. They have plenty of detractors, but you should consider using these highly visible miniature ads to make your initial contact with potential customers. A good banner ad will create instant awareness of your site, and you can select a targeted plan that shows your ad only to prospects who click on related subjects.

When you write a banner ad, keep it brief and make it snappy. Include the command "Click Here" at the bottom of the banner, even though it seems obvious—that's your call to action. Display your Web address as well, just to impress it into the visitor's consciousness with repeat viewings. That doesn't leave you much room for copy. But animated banner ads can give you two or three shots at saying something memorable.

Customers who respond to your ad will be receptive to your subsequent E-mail offers and/or newsletters. There's no better way to gather names for opt-in mailings (as opposed to unsolicited spam). That's the polite way to do business online.

Compare the different payment plans for banner ads, estimate a 2 percent click-through response, and measure the cost of driving a customer to your site against the anticipated lifetime value of that customer. If you have any doubts, remember that there are less expensive ways to find customers.

E-Mail Newsletters. *One of the most effective and inexpensive media ever developed for nurturing a relationship with your customers.*

I don't think I'm overstating the case for E-mail newsletters. You're providing informative content your customers look forward to reading, and you can relax into a chatty, offbeat, low-pressure style of communication that you can't afford to try in your catalogs or direct-mail packages.

Your offers appear almost incidental to the newsletter content—but they're still prominently displayed and linked to your site. Best of all, the customer who has been engrossed in your newsletter will be far more receptive to your ad than someone you've just dragged in from cyberspace.

You can easily personalize your newsletters, test different offers, and gain new readers through customer referrals. Sounds almost too good to be true, doesn't it?

The challenge is to keep coming up with interesting new content in each issue. (Somebody has to find the time to sit down and do the actual writing.) At my previous company, we used to invite readers to submit their own "true tales" about their experiences with our products. These stories turned out to have tremendous entertainment value, and they made my writing job *a lot* easier.

Invite your customers to contribute content to your newsletter. You might even approach some of the rising stars in your field to write occasional articles at no charge. If your circulation is impressive enough, they'll do it for the free career publicity (and a link to their own site).

E-Mail Sales Letters. *The last refuge of long copy in the electronic age.*

Pay no attention to the experts who caution you against lengthy online messages. A well-crafted sales letter is the exception to the rule. Everyone loves a good story told with gusto—especially if it clearly leads to some tangible benefits.

Granted, today's video-conditioned prospects tend to skim more than they read. But if you can snag your readers with a compelling (and truthful) subject line, an irresistible offer, and a magnetic message, they're yours for the duration. Try to make the body of your letter as informative and involving as possible; an unrelieved sales pitch won't work online any more than it does on paper.

E-mail sales letters offer a few improvements over the old-fashioned paper-and-ink variety. They're cheap to create. You don't have to pay for postage. They can link directly to the offer page on your site. (What better response vehicle could you imagine?) And think of all the innocent trees you'll be saving.

True, you have to overcome the spam resistance so prevalent among online prospects and even "smart" E-mail programs like Microsoft Outlook (which automatically classifies ad messages as spam). Your response rate probably won't match what you could achieve with a mailed package. But if you weigh that lower response rate against the vast extra quantities you can mail at virtually no cost, you still come out ahead.

If you have qualms about sending unsolicited E-mail, gather your own list of prospects who click on your banner ads or register at your site. You won't have to worry about the spam police, and your response rate should skyrocket.

E-Mail Subject Lines. *The verbal nudge that prompts the recipient to open your E-mail message.*

So many of these "grabbers" are blatant (and willfully deceptive) come-ons that they've probably damaged the credibility of E-mail advertising for the next generation. I wish I had saved a few dozen of the more preposterous subject lines I've read over the years—greetings like "I tried to call you last night," "I'm hot for you, baby," and, of course, "Here's the information you requested." (Yeah, right.)

These unsavory mountebanks have their reasons for trying to sneak in under the radar. After all, most of us delete obvious advertising E-mails before we even open them. (You know the problem: spam, spam, spam, spam!) These online advertisers feel they have to disguise their E-mails as personal correspondence. To me, that's a sign of desperation.

I challenge you to create an E-mail subject line that sings to the reader but doesn't conceal its purpose. Think carefully, use words frugally, make your message original and irresistible—but keep it honest. (You can make it a benefit, an offer, or a personal invitation—as long as it relates to the content of your E-mail.)

After all, if your subject line is revealed as a sham after the reader opens the E-mail and skims the first few lines, you can be sure your prospect will delete your brainchild forthwith. You may have gained a name for your list, but you've lost a customer.

Pop-Up Ads. *Pesky messages that materialize from out of nowhere when you click on a link.*

Everybody hates 'em. Nobody reads 'em. Don't create 'em. 'Nuff said.

Press Releases. *Self-generated news articles that could generate free publicity for your product, company, or site.*

You can write your own electronic press releases and E-mail them to selected media addresses that you've looked up and targeted. Or you can use the services of an online promoter and pay to have it written and/or E-mailed to the right places. Some of these companies claim to have more clout than you when it comes to getting your story placed. I'd be a bit skeptical, but it couldn't hurt to look into established services like Business Wire or PR Newswire.

If you write your own release, the first point to remember is that your story must sound like news. The editor who reads it is looking for story material, and an overzealous puff piece won't cut it.

Use the traditional "inverted pyramid" approach to writing your story: important information at the top, less important information toward the bottom. Online press releases tend to be shorter than the printed variety—two-thirds of a page is typical. Make your points quickly and forcefully, and let the editor round out your press release into a full-bodied story.

A press release that hits the mark can find its way into print magazines and newspapers as well as online news media. The results can drive your traffic into the stratosphere with virtually no expenditure on your part. If at first you don't succeed, try again. And again. And again. You have nothing to lose.

Web Copy. *Your booth at that great desktop bazaar known as the World Wide Web.*

What a gift the Web has turned out to be! Companies can set up shop and broadcast their wares at minimal cost. Customers can zero in on just the products and services that interest them—without having to sift through a hefty catalog and without ever budging from their desks. And they can reach you twenty-four hours a day, every day of the year (including weekends and holidays).

During the early heyday of the Web in the 1990s, site design seemed to focus on bells and whistles as much as content. Everyone competed to see who could create the coolest and most innovative site. Now that the dust has cleared, it's obvious that you need compelling content (as well as easy navigation) to keep your visitors coming back for more.

Write for an impatient audience; reader boredom is fatal. Keep your sentences relatively short and muscular, especially on the home page. Use enough subheads to aid rapid scanning, but not so many that you clutter the screen with them. Make your graphics serve the copy and not vice versa.

The Web is a visual medium, but it's primarily a written one. Yet somewhere along the way, the idea of a distinctive company "voice"—such a powerful factor in print advertising and catalogs—seems to have been lost in the shuffle. So many company sites come across as bland and institutional, almost interchangeable. The writing seems to have been created by committee.

The Web phrases I've provided in this book will help you add useful features to your site and call attention to them. But you have to breathe life into your site through what you write. If you want your site to become a traffic magnet, make sure you write it with heart, personality, and conviction. Know who you are, and don't try to sound like everyone else. Think of your site not only as an electronic store, but as the ultimate tool for creating a recognizable brand personality that stands out from the competition.

FURTHER READING

Bayan, Richard. *Words That Sell: A Thesaurus to Help Promote Your Products, Services, and Ideas*. Chicago: Contemporary Books, 1987.

> The original advertising thesaurus, still a popular reference tool for people who write their own copy. Indispensable companion to the more specialized *More Words That Sell*, filled with words and phrases you can use in all forms of advertising and promotion.

Bly, Robert W. *Copywriter's Handbook: A Step-by-Step Guide to Writing Copy That Sells*. New York: Henry Holt, 1990.

> Very solid (if marginally outdated) step-by-step guide to the fundamentals of creating effective copy. For print advertising techniques, you can't go wrong with this book.

Caples, John. *Tested Advertising Methods*. Updated by Fred E. Hahn. 5th ed. Paramus, N.J.: Prentice-Hall, 1997.

> Don't let the lackluster title fool you. This is possibly the finest book of its kind ever written, and its author was a legendary pioneer of direct-mail advertising. Timeless wisdom on the psychology and techniques of copywriting for measurable results.

Dahl, Gary. *Advertising for Dummies*. New York: Hungry Minds, 2001.

> Essential, easy-to-absorb information for do-it-yourselfers. Good introduction to the business side of advertising, but weak on copywriting.

Glazier, Stephen. *Random House Webster's Word Menu*. Revised ed. New York: Random House, 1998.

Nearly a thousand pages of word lists organized by category, originally compiled by one heroic man. A staggering achievement, great for leisurely browsing as well as quick look-ups.

Godin, Seth. *Permission Marketing: Turning Strangers into Friends and Friends into Customers*. New York: Simon and Schuster, 1999.

A thoughtful, influential guide to opt-in marketing on the Internet.

Hatch, Denny, and Don Jackson. *2,239 Tested Secrets for Direct Marketing Success: The Pros Tell You Their Time-Proven Secrets*. Lincolnwood, Ill.: NTC Business Books, 1998.

Anyone who writes direct-response copy can profit from this handy bag of tricks.

Hatch, Denny. *Million Dollar Mailings: The Art and Science of Creating Money-Making Direct Mail*. Chicago: Bonus Books, 2001.

Expensive but invaluable in-depth look at actual direct-mail winners and what they did right. See if you can find it in the library or persuade your company to purchase it.

Kennedy, Dan S. *The Ultimate Sales Letter: Boost Your Sales with Powerful Sales Letters, Based on Madison Avenue Techniques*. Holbrook, Mass.: Adams Media Corp., 2000.

Highly regarded primer on crafting sales letters that hit the mark. Not just a compilation of examples, though it includes lots of them.

Lewis, Herschell Gordon. *Catalog Copy That Sizzles: All the Hints, Tips, and Tricks of the Trade You'll Need to Write Copy That Sells*. Lincolnwood, Ill.: NTC Business Books, 2000.

Lewis, Herschell Gordon. *Direct Mail Copy That Sells!* Englewood Cliffs, NJ: Prentice Hall, 1984.

Lewis, Herschell Gordon. *On the Art of Writing Copy: The Best of * Print * Broadcast * Internet * Direct Mail*. New York: AMACOM, 2000.

Lewis is a fascinating contradiction: a maverick spirit who promotes strict adherence to the rules. He habitually lambastes other people's defective copy but still emerges as an insightful, amusing, and very sound teacher. I've listed just a few of his twenty or so books.

Macpherson, Kim. *Permission-Based E-Mail Marketing That Works!* Chicago: Dearborn Trade Publishing, 2001.

Practical tips for aspiring online entrepreneurs—ideal in combination with Seth Godin's more conceptual *Permission Marketing*.

Ogilvy, David. *Ogilvy on Advertising*. New York: Vintage Books, 1987.

Classic advice and insights from the late Madison Avenue legend. Not for agency copywriters only.

Ries, Al, and Jack Trout. *Positioning: The Battle for Your Mind*. New York: McGraw-Hill, 2001.

An influential work that shows you how to make your product or company stand out from the crowd.

Roget's 21st Century Thesaurus in Dictionary Form: The Essential Reference for Home, School, or Office. Edited by the Princeton Language Institute. 2d ed. New York: Dell, 1999.

When you can't find what you need in my *Words That Sell* books, turn to this indispensable compendium of synonyms. Going strong since 1852, the venerable Roget's has been updated with a special concept index that makes it even more useful.

Schwab, Victor O. *How to Write a Good Advertisement*. North Hollywood, Calif.: Wilshire, 1985.

A pre-Internet classic that's simply too good to ignore. Truth never needs to be revised.

Strunk, William, and E. B. White. *The Elements of Style.* 4th ed. Boston: Allyn & Bacon, 2000.

This slim, ageless reference guide to English usage and composition was recently updated. Every writer should own it and use it.

Sugarman, Joseph. *Advertising Secrets of the Written Word: The Ultimate Resource on How to Write Powerful Advertising Copy from One of America's Top Copywriters and Mail Order Entrepreneurs.* Las Vegas: Delstar, 1998.

Need I say more? A popular guide that covers everything you'd want to know. It's not cheap, so see if your company will order it for you.

Sugarman, Joe. *Triggers: 30 Sales Tools You Can Use to Control the Mind of Your Prospect to Motivate, Influence, and Persuade.* Las Vegas: Delstar, 1999.

Another worthwhile book with a long subtitle from the same marketing mastermind.

Trout, Jack, with Steve Rivkin. *Differentiate or Die: Survival in Our Era of Killer Competition.* New York: Wiley, 2000.

More about the art of positioning your product or company to establish a unique identity.

Trout, Jack, with Steve Rivkin. *The New Postioning: The Latest on the World's #1 Business Strategy.* New York: McGraw-Hill, 1996.

Follow-up to *Positioning*, with emphasis on repositioning in response to change.

Usborne, Nick. *Net Words: Creating High-Impact Online Copy.* New York: McGraw-Hill, 2002.

Intelligent, in-depth advice on how to shape your writing for the Internet. Not a quick-reference tool, but well worth a read.

Werz, Edward, and Sally Germain. *Phrases That Sell: The Ultimate Phrase Finder to Help You Promote Your Products, Services, and Ideas.* Lincolnwood, Ill.: Contemporary Books, 1998.

Clearly a *Words That Sell* wannabe, but still a useful reference book if you want to expand your repertoire of promotional phrases. Just make sure you buy *Words That Sell* first!